MW00588230

presented to

_____

from

_____

date

_____

pass it on

A PROVERBS JOURNAL FOR THE NEXT GENERATION

Champ Thornton

New
Growth
Press

www.newgrowthpress.com

New Growth Press, Greensboro, NC 27404
Copyright © 2017 George Thomas Thornton II

All rights reserved. No part of this publication may be reproduced, stored in a retrieval system, or transmitted in any form by any means, electronic, mechanical, photocopy, recording, or otherwise, without the prior permission of the publisher, except as provided by USA copyright law.

Primary Proverbs translation is taken from Bruce Waltke, "The Book of Proverbs: Chapters 1–15" in *The New International Commentary on the Old Testament* (Grand Rapids: Wm. B. Eerdmans, 2004) and Bruce Waltke, "The Book of Proverbs: Chapters 15–31" in *The New International Commentary on the Old Testament* (Grand Rapids: Wm. B. Eerdmans, 2005).

Scripture quotations are taken from The Holy Bible, English Standard Version.® Copyright © 2000; 2001 by Crossway Bibles, a division of Good News Publishers. Used by permission. All rights reserved.

Scripture quotations marked NIV are taken from THE HOLY BIBLE, NEW INTERNATIONAL VERSION®, NIV® Copyright © 1973, 1978, 1984, 2011 by Biblica, Inc.® Used by permission. All rights reserved worldwide.

Scripture quotations marked NLT are taken from the Holy Bible, New Living Translation, copyright ©1996, 2004, 2007 by Tyndale House Foundation. Used by permission of Tyndale House Publishers, Inc., Carol Stream, Illinois 60188. All rights reserved.

Scripture quotations noted KJV are from The Holy Bible: King James Version.

Cover Design: Faceout Books, faceoutstudio.com

ISBN 978-1-945270-78-9

Printed in China

24 23 22 21 20 19 18 17   1 2 3 4 5

Contents

For my fathers, in family and in faith,
who still teach me about life and about God:
George Thornton and Eric Sipe

How to Use This Journal

My wife and I have the joy and responsibility to prepare our three children for life in the real world. Since our children were little, I have desired to teach them the godly wisdom found in Proverbs. But I knew that I needed to grow in my own understanding of Proverbs before I could pass it on to my family. That need led to years of study, which led in turn to this book: my attempt to capture Proverb's wisdom for the benefit of the next generation. Proverbs-filled children come from Proverbs-filled parents.

Learn and Share

Using this journal will help you to learn and apply this wisdom-saturated portion of God's Word to your daily life. Once you finish filling its pages with your notes, insights, and memories, you can share it by giving your journal away—perhaps to a child, grandchild, nephew, niece, or a young friend. By doing this you will be passing on a legacy of wisdom to be treasured for generations.

In this journal you'll find plenty of space for you to add your own notes both on Proverbs and on the wisdom you've gained from life experiences. While the first is inspired and the second is not, both are, to differing degrees, valuable. So, write down your observations, prayers, encouragements, and counsel for the next generation. Let the words of Proverbs prompt you to retell your story, recounting how God has been faithful to you through your life.

There are thirty-two sections to complete, so if you use the journal for ten minutes each day, your personalized book will be ready to give away in just a few months. But don't get too worried about how much time it takes. The main thing is to just keep going, bit by bit, learning and sharing something each day.

Start by asking God to help you as you read and journal. Pray that he will open your eyes to the beauty and truth of what he has written, so that you can *pass it on* to the next generation (Psalm 119:18).

Here is a quick overview of what you will find in the journal and how to use each section.

1. **Read "A Bird's-Eye View of Proverbs" before you start the journal.** This will give you an overview of Proverbs and help to orient and inform your reading.

2. **Read the Guided Tour before you begin each chapter of Proverbs.** These notes will help you understand the chapter you're studying. Mark the text of Proverbs accordingly (e.g., if the Guided Tour states that 3:13–20 describe the benefits of wisdom, you could mark those verses, labeling them as "Benefits").

3. **Study one chapter of Proverbs per week (or take longer).** As short, memorable encapsulations of wisdom, individual proverbs were meant to be savored piece by piece, not all devoured in one sitting. So prayerfully read and think about one chapter at a time.

   The fresh and careful translation provided comes from Dr. Bruce Waltke, who, now in his eighties, has devoted his life to a humble and Christ-focused study of God's Word, and especially the book of Proverbs. His two-volume work on Proverbs is considered by many as the premier commentary in the English language. As you study the translation of individual chapters, add your own comments in the margins. And feel free to circle, underline, and connect key words or phrases as you see them in the chapter for the day.

4. **Complete the "Reflections" section.** This section gives you the opportunity to write down your thoughts and observations about the proverbs you are studying and also to share your own insights and experiences with the next generation. Each section contains the following:

   Identifying a Verse – Record your thoughts about a verse that stood out to you.
   Going Deeper – Reflect on portions of each chapter by answering the questions provided.
   Connecting the Gospel – Consider how the wisdom of Proverbs relates to the grace and gospel of Jesus Christ.
   Personalizing a Prayer – Transform the truth and encouragement that you have learned from Proverbs into a personalized prayer for

the journal's final owner. If you are not sure how to begin, here's a classic four-part pattern that you could use:

- **The Person** (What do you learn about God in that chapter of Proverbs that helps shape your prayer? E.g., "Father, you are all-wise . . .")
- **The Petition** (Based on something from Proverbs, what is a prayer request you're making for the final owner of this journal?)
- **The Purpose** (Using some desirable outcome expressed in Proverbs, what are you hoping that your request may accomplish?)
- **The Plea** (All Christian prayer is offered "in Jesus's name": on the basis of Christ's merits, not our own.)[1]

Sharing Your Story – Here is your chance to answer questions about yourself and share your faith story with the next generation. You can also record your observations of how and where you see the final owner of this journal already living out some portion of the chapter you just read in Proverbs. Use concrete examples and be generous with your words of encouragement. If you want, you can be even more creative in this section—think about drawing a picture (it's worth a thousand words!), sketching a diagram, or even writing a poem. Whoever receives this journal will treasure whatever you do.

5. **Give this Proverbs journal to its final owner.**[2]

A Bird's-Eye View of Proverbs

Proverbs is a treasure chest of wisdom that sits unlocked right in the middle of the Bible. The book you're holding presents an invitation to open the lid, scoop out its wealth, and pass it on to the next generation—a legacy of wisdom.

This is no small task as the sheer size of this treasure (thirty-one chapters—915 verses!) makes clear. The difficulty mounts when you realize that about two-thirds of the book seem to be individual, stand-alone pieces of advice: 600-something pearls of wisdom rolling around unstrung. Yet isn't this how life unfolds? A never-ending cascade of unrelated events tumbling toward us. Proverbs mirrors the seemingly random arrangement of life. Real-life wisdom for real-life situations.

The challenge is to make every part of this treasure our own. Then we can live in wisdom and help our children do the same. For this bounty exists not for hoarding but sharing. Such a treasure trove of wisdom makes a priceless inheritance for any generation to pass down to the next.

Riches await. But where to start digging?

Let's start with an overview of Proverbs—a bird's-eye look at how it's put together and how all those small gems of wisdom hang together on common threads of truth. Don't skip this part! Using a wide-angle lens will prove invaluable to you as you examine the details of the book of Proverbs.

The Structure of Proverbs

Proverbs contains the following six collections of short, usually two-line proverbs. These six main sections are framed by two bookends: a long prologue on the need for wisdom (1:1–9:18) and an epilogue on an example of wisdom (31:10–31).

Proverbs of Solomon I	(10:1—22:16)
Sayings of the Wise I	(22:17—24:22)
Sayings of the Wise II	(24:23–34)
Proverbs of Solomon II	(25:1—29:27)
Sayings of Agur	(30:1–33)
Sayings of Lemuel	(31:1–31)

Organized according to its content, the book of Proverbs divides neatly into two sections: chapters 1–9 and chapters 10–31. Both these divisions encourage wise living but differ in their purpose and format.

SEEK WISDOM (CHAPTERS 1–9)

The first section (chapters 1–9), encourages the pursuit of wisdom, preparing the reader for the second section (chapters 10–31). In summary, chapters 1–9 aim to motivate the reader to seek wisdom, while also avoiding foolish men and forbidden women.

Fifteen times, the older generation speaks directly to the younger—calling, imploring, enticing. Here's a sampling: "Hear, my son" (Proverbs 1:8); "My son, do not forget my teaching" (3:1); "My son, be attentive to my words" (4:20); "Then do this, my son, and save yourself" (6:3); "My son, keep my words and treasure up my commandments" (7:1).[3]

When, in these examples, Proverbs records a father's wisdom being passed on to his son, the historic "father" in view is Solomon (or one of the other inspired authors listed in endnote 12). And since Proverbs is part of God's Word, this collected wisdom may also apply as God-given parental advice to sons in any generation. However, Hebrews 12:5–7 further broadens those addressed in Proverbs as "sons" to include all of God's "sons" (and daughters) and also identifies the father who speaks as God himself. So in Proverbs we should hear more than the advice of good fathers; we should also hear the voice of God the Father. Proverbs is God's wise instruction to all his children.

Not surprisingly, then, the first nine chapters contain numerous statements of fatherly advice. Yet instead of immediately beginning to teach wisdom itself, chapters 1–9 primarily feature incentives for becoming wise: reminders to pursue wisdom, blessings for gaining wisdom, and warnings about refusing wisdom. Here's a sampling of these elements from each of the first nine chapters.

Reminders	Blessings	Warnings
1:8	1:9	1:19
2:1	2:10–11	2:22
3:1	3:13–14	3:32–35
4:1–2	4:8–9	4:19
5:1	5:2	5:23
6:20–21	6:22–24	6:26–35
7:1–4	7:5	7:26–27
8:5–7	8:18–21	8:36
9:4–6	9:11	9:12

The first nine chapters lay out argument after argument and reason after reason, to convince the reader that the path of wisdom is the best road to travel. In this way, the first section (chapters 1–9) serves to introduce the second section (chapters 10–31). To change the metaphor from a treasure to a feast, chapters 1–9 whet the appetite and set the table. Chapters 10–31 serve the food.

FIND WISDOM (CHAPTERS 10–31)

The second and largest section of Proverbs features concise observations about how life works best. This section features wise words wisely written.

Most commonly in this section, these short proverbs come in the form of a two-line poem or couplet.[4] They are gems of wisdom, often sparkling with vivid wording and striking imagery which make them both beautiful and memorable.

Sometimes these proverbs *commend*. Functionally, they prescribe a wise direction: they tell what you should do. Here are some examples of these prescriptive proverbs.

> Commit your work to the LORD, and your plans will be established. (16:3)

Do not exploit the poor because they are poor, and do not crush the needy in court. (22:22 NIV)

Other times, individual proverbs *observe*. Functionally, they describe God's wise design: they tell what is true. Consider these examples of descriptive proverbs:

The LORD has made everything for its purpose, even the wicked for the day of trouble. (16:4)

The lot is cast into the lap, but its every decision is from the LORD. (16:33)

Nearly every one of the 659 verses in chapters 10–31 nicely fits one of these two functions: prescriptive or descriptive. Yet beyond these two categories, the order and arrangement of proverbs initially seem somewhat random, following no orderly pattern. The topics addressed are diverse: anger, laziness, planning, gossip, friendship, love, self-control, eating, politics, family, and money. Again, the apparent disorder of the structure mimics the unpredictable rush of everyday life.

However, on closer observation of chapters 10–31, particular topics seem to cluster loosely together. For example, about one-third of the verses in chapter 21 deals with money; over 60% of the verses in chapter 18 talk about words; and the first half of chapter 10 alternates between the topics of words and wealth, while the last half mentions, in nearly every verse, the consequences of one's actions.

Then, like short strands of pearls, there are other passages that seem united even more closely along a single idea. Here are some samples of these topically arranged blocks of verses.

10:2–5 addresses wealth and poverty

15:1–4 deals mostly with speech

15:33–16:9 features repeated references to the Lord

16:10–15 focuses attention on the king

16:20–23 specifically discusses wisdom

18:4–8 gives advice about communication

23:29–35 explains the problems with drunkenness

24:30–34 gives teaching on laziness

25:1–15 seems to describe wise living in a king's court

26:3–12 repeatedly speaks of the nature of fools

26:13–16 warns against sluggards

27:23–27 gives wise counsel about caring for "flocks of sheep"

31:1–9 provides advice for being a noble king

31:10–31 paints the portrait of an ideal wife

You can find additional details about the arrangement of themes within Proverbs, in the "Guided Tour" before each chapter. You will read and understand Proverbs better by knowing its structure. But what about the actual content of Proverbs?

WORLDVIEW OF PROVERBS

Although the structure of Proverbs follows a generally loose arrangement, its overall message is tight and cohesive. This unified outlook is its "worldview."[5] A worldview has been described as "a set of presuppositions . . . that we hold (consciously or unconsciously) about the basic constitution of reality."

So, while presenting dozens of different topics, the perspective of Proverbs never changes—just as a bird watcher, who sits in one spot, may observe an entire forest of color, sound, smells, and motion. This unchanging "spot" or worldview of Proverbs reveals a unified view of life.

This means that for Proverbs the "wise person" doesn't just memorize and execute a tidy collection of good advice.[6] True wisdom is living in light of what's real, in awareness of the actual make-up of our world.[7] The major realities of Proverb's worldview are (1) a wise and powerful God, (2) a wisely designed and orderly creation, (3) the divergent pathways of wise and foolish humans, and (4) the consequences of their respective choices.

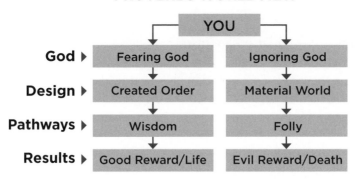

GOD

The foremost reality in the universe is God himself. Proverbs reminds us that living wisely in God's world starts with living in "the fear of the LORD" (1:7; 9:10). Living in the fear of the LORD means that you are constantly aware that he is God and you are not; that he is BIG and you are small.[8] Who is this God?

The "LORD" referred to in these verses (and eighty-six additional times within the book of Proverbs) is different than the generic designation: "God" (five times in Proverbs). Instead, "LORD" is the English translation of Yahweh (or Jehovah), referring to the faithful, covenant-keeping God who has lovingly committed himself to his people. When God signs an agreement with his people (and when he speaks to them words of fatherly wisdom), "LORD" is the name he uses (Exodus 3:14–15; 6:2–3, 6–8).

Additionally, this LORD created everything (Proverbs 3:19–20; 8:26–31; 22:2, 12), provides everything (2:6–8, 3:11; 8:22; 10:22; 18:22; 21:31), knows everything (5:21; 16:2; 21:2; 24:18), judges everything (3:11–12; 5:21; 6:16–19), and rules everything (16:1–9; 19:21; 20:24; 21:1, 31; 29:26).

If, in contrast to fearing the LORD, you minimize him—if you act like there is no God—then you're going to live foolishly. You will be ignoring the most massive and prevalent reality in the universe—to your own peril. To live on planet earth while acting as if there were no God is like walking around with your eyes shut. You can certainly do it, but you're going to get pretty banged up.[9]

The wisdom of Proverbs may illuminate the right path you should walk, but only a pervasive awareness of God ("fear of the LORD") will actually keep you on that road. God himself is the starting place for men and women wanting to be wise in their view of the world.

DESIGN

The second reality underlying Proverbs is that God made the world in a wise way, according to a wise design (3:19–20). A quick read through the first few chapters of Genesis will show that God didn't just slap dash the universe together. Instead, there is order and wisdom in all that he made. Proverbs agrees:

> I [wisdom] was the architect at his side. I was his constant delight, rejoicing always in his presence. (Proverbs 8:30 NLT)

God made the world wisely. His own wisdom guided his creating. The word translated "architect" has also been rendered "craftsman," or even "blueprint." This is "divine wisdom, God's plan or order, 'wrought into the constitution of the universe.'"[10]

An Orderly Design

This means that God designed his created world to operate according to certain consistent and orderly patterns. For example, there is a physical order—if you jump off a cliff, it will likely be the last unwise decision you make. And there is a moral order—if you gossip, you will probably lose friends.

These patterns don't change. They are constants, applying to all people, cultures, and eras of history. God's order is hardwired into the world, woven into the fabric of creation. So, when we live in harmony with his original design, we mirror God's wisdom. That is, we ourselves are being wise.

An Observable Design

The universe God made is not only orderly (people can set their watches by it), but it is also knowable (people have learned how to set their watches by it). We can appreciate the structures and designs of God's world by observing what he created.

God expects us to notice patterns and traits in the world around us. This is wisdom acquired by us firsthand. We are supposed to notice and learn from broken-down walls (25:28), industrious ants (6:6), table arrangements (23:1), fast-talking fools (29:20), and exemplary parents (23:26).[11] And throughout this journal, you will have space to pass on this kind of wisdom—personal observations gained over the course of your life.

Additionally, we should also become wise through listening to the sage observation of others. This is secondhand wisdom. Proverbs repeatedly insists we take heed to our teachers (5:13), to our parents (23:22), and to the divinely inspired authors of Proverbs themselves (1:1–6; 23:12).[12]

Whether learning from observations or from others, wise men and women must seek to rightly understand and rightly relate to God's orderly world. The only alternative is foolishness: to ignore God and invent a self-customized plan for living. Pursuing either folly or wisdom, all human beings must walk one path or the other.

PATHWAYS

Turn to any portion of Proverbs and you will be confronted with a fork in the road: Will you take the pathway of wisdom or the pathway of folly? Though Proverbs addresses dozens of topics, its thirty-one chapters actually present every reader with only two routes through life: the wise way or the foolish way.

The Pathway of Folly

Proverbs employs a rich vocabulary to set forth both the value of wisdom in all her beauty and also the horror of folly in all her lunacy. This variety reminds us that not all fools are the same. The simple immaturity of a three-year-old doesn't compare to the selfish recklessness of a twenty-one-year-old—and each kind of person deserves his own fool-appropriate response. Proverbs wisely recognizes these differences (1:22). It distinguishes progressive stages along the downhill path of folly, identifying three different kinds of people: the Immature, the Fool, and the Mocker.

1. The Immature—an experientially naïve person

The first steps along the path of folly belong to the simpleton. This person is irresponsible and untrained. Loving his immaturity, this person has no experiences in life to warn him of the dangers that lie along the path ahead (Proverbs 27:12). If this person is left undirected, the magnetic pull of rebellion against God will draw him ever closer toward destruction (22:3). He or she is vulnerable and uncommitted regarding wisdom (neither for nor against it), and is therefore still teachable (19:25; 21:11). When addressing these kinds of "rookie fools," teachers should seek both to educate them about God's orderly ways in this world (1:4) and also to warn them about ignoring his ways . . . lest they become an outright fool.

2. The Fool—a spiritually thickheaded person

The next downward phase is the most common: a garden-variety fool. He is not simply stupid or naïve but actually refuses to listen to the wisdom of parents and counselors (Proverbs 12:15). This disobedient person has whipped up his own home-cooked version of what he supposes to be "wisdom" (1:29). Unwilling to learn, this person may, however, be turned toward wisdom when consequences are enforced (8:5; 19:29; 26:5). Humanly speaking, painful correction may be the only thing that gets through his thick skull . . . and keeps him from the worst stage of all.

3. The Mocker—a willfully independent person

This arrogant person doesn't just refuse to listen; he actually despises the wisdom of God. He hates any attempts to correct his actions or thinking (Proverbs 9:7–18; 13:1; 15:12). The gullibility of the Immature and the resistance of the Fool are gone. What remains is outright antagonism toward God's ways and sheer delight in that rebellion (1:22). This settled and arrogant independence makes movement back toward wisdom practically, though not entirely, impossible (14:6). He receives no benefit from discipline (9:7), rebuke (9:8; 15:12), or instruction (13:1). Unless he turns from his own "wisdom" and submits to God's wisdom, the Mocker will find, all too late, that the pathway of folly dead-ends in destruction. But there is another way.

The Pathway of Wisdom

What is the biblical concept of wisdom? A wise person knows how God has made the world to work and skillfully shapes his life to go with (not against) the grain of God's creation.[13] Proverbs views wisdom as skill in relationships—living in right relationship with the realities of God's good and orderly, but fallen and chaotic universe.[14] This includes properly relating to God, other people, the created world, and one's self.

Of course, thriving in these relationships doesn't happen overnight. The pathway of wisdom is walked, not sprinted. So it shouldn't be a surprise that the process of learning God's ways in his orderly world has a definite beginning, a desired ending, and many steps in between. Thankfully, God has described these stages for us. Proverbs 2:1–10, one of the most orderly and structured passages in the entire book, maps out this march toward wisdom.

1. Accept the Wisdom You Have (2:1–2)

According to Proverbs 2, the naïve or untrained person must first willingly receive the wisdom of his instructors (parents, teachers, etc.). Notice how in these first two verses, he simply welcomes wisdom from others: "accept," "store up," "make your ear attentive," "apply your heart toward understanding."

This first phase implies active teaching by the mentor and active listening by the learner. If you are a parent, don't forget that God has already provided your child with his first building block to be wise: you! This requires that you must be wise yourself—knowing and living in harmony with God's created and moral order. And to then impart this wisdom to your child, you must talk, talk, talk, teach, teach, teach. The next generation takes their first steps on the road toward wisdom by accepting the wise instruction of others.

2. Seek the Wisdom You Lack (2:3–4)

According to Solomon, the next piece of wise instruction a child must accept is this: "Start seeking wisdom yourself." Those who accept the wisdom of others should not become content to be spoon-fed by others. They must also start praying that God would give them the wisdom they don't yet have. This kind of prayer plays a vital role in the treasure hunt for wisdom, whose value exceeds gold or silver (Proverbs 3:14).

As a parent, you should encourage your child to ask God for the skill needed to make wise choices. You can also provide a model of asking by praying with your child for the wisdom he or she needs. If someone lacks wisdom, he should expectantly ask God to meet that need (James 1:5). For he is the Source of true wisdom, and he generously gives wisdom to those who seek it.

3. Gain the Wisdom You Need (2:5–8)

The next two verses lay out the next step toward wisdom. What is sought and requested in Proverbs 2:3–4, is found in 2:5–6 and enjoyed in 2:7–8. When the Lord hears requests for wisdom, he answers by giving the elements required to get wisdom. He gives "the fear of the Lord," which is the prerequisite for living wisely, and he also begins to give out some beginner's skills in wise living (2:5–6).

A child living in the "fear of the Lord" begins to factor the reality of God into his own perceptions of life. His eyes start to open to a new reality of life: God himself. Alongside the fear of God, also comes some initial wisdom from God. And any who gain this wisdom will begin to benefit from this wisdom (2:7–8).[15]

4. Internalize the Wisdom You Know (2:9–10)

Retracing the flow of thought begun in Proverbs 2:1, the first step away from folly requires simply accepting the wisdom of others (Proverbs 2:1–2). The next step starts one's own personal quest to seek wisdom from God (2:3–4). The third step (2:5–8) gains the ingredients required for wisdom: the fear of the Lord and wise teaching from his mouth. And now the fourth step goes even further.

Proverbs 2:9 says that after you've received God's wisdom, you will understand "every good track [or path]." The reason for such comprehensive and mature insight is that wisdom has now come to reside deep inside you, in your heart. And this internalized wisdom not only guides but also changes you, so that you actually enjoy God's wise ways (2:10).

In the first three steps outlined in Proverbs 2:1–8, wisdom mainly exists outside the learner or child: in the wisdom of teachers, parents, or even God himself. But a child reaches the height of wisdom when the skill learned from others actually becomes her own. A wise person is not one who has merely mastered wisdom, but who has been mastered by it.

*****

Wisdom, then, is not just gaining familiarity with a list of proverbs but internalizing a versatile approach to life. Situations will arise in life that Proverbs never addresses. In these cases, the book of Proverbs serves as a starter kit, teaching a worldview that can adapt skillfully to new and unfamiliar challenges. You begin learning Proverbs like reading a map, exploring each square foot of its 915 verses. Yet, as you internalize its wisdom, the map becomes a compass, enabling you to navigate any terrain you encounter.[16]

Or to switch the metaphor, any orator may learn to speak by looking at the words on the teleprompter, but a skilled public speaker sees the words and looks through the teleprompter adapting to the audience before him. Similarly, our view of Proverbs changes as Proverbs changes us. The more you see the ways of God's world in it, the more you may see his world through it.[17]

This means that God intends that you not only learn the wisdom found in Proverbs, but also build on it by making your own observations. A friend of mine often expresses this truth with the helpful reminder: "Read your environment." Wise people learn to live skillfully despite the ever-changing situations encountered. That's why there is space in the "Reflections" sections throughout this journal where you can add your own words of wisdom.

RESULTS

Finally, the worldview of Proverbs includes the consequences of choices. Because we live in God's wisely ordered universe, the destinations of our path—the results of our choices—are somewhat predictable.

Like a reliable map, Proverbs lays out the connections, which in a God-ordered universe, exist between pathways and destinations, between choices and consequences. If you follow the map of wisdom, your wise choices usually lead to good results, while foolish choices typically lead to bad results. Deeds lead to destiny. Or you could say it this way: If you do good? You'll get good. Do evil? Get evil. Not uncommonly these outcomes are described in terms of either "life" (Proverbs 3:2, 16, 18,

22; 4:13, etc.) or "death" (2:18; 5:5; 8:36; 14:12; 16:25; etc.). Wise living, according to Proverbs, leads to life and blessing, while folly leads to death and disaster.[18]

Of course, Proverbs itself teaches that this kind of formulaic construction isn't the entire story. Each individual proverb presents only part of God's reality for this world, not its entirety. For example, in some cases the righteous experience poverty (Proverbs 15:16); while other scenarios find righteousness rewarded with prosperity (12:27).

Yet more than this, the Bible as a whole teaches that there are exceptions to the deed-destiny connections mapped out in Proverbs: uncharted areas beyond the ability of human beings to comprehend or predict. The Bible acknowledges that on this fallen planet, sometimes choices and results seem connected unjustly (cf. the book of Job) and sometimes choices and results seem related nonsensically (cf. the book of Ecclesiastes). These two books are the wild, wild west of God's Word. They don't present the neat and tidy, cause-and-effect patterns of God's moral universe, which are so often affirmed throughout the book of Proverbs. Job and Ecclesiastes (and the life of Christ) show us that there is more to God's plans than neat and tidy outcomes. You have probably experienced that in your life as well. But that doesn't take away from the wisdom to be found in Proverbs. God's world usually follows a pattern where wise choices result in blessing for those who make them.[19] And, of course, the most amazing blessing is found in Christ (Ephesians 1:3): becoming a child of God, following the Savior, and bearing the fruit of his Spirit.

Given the realities of Job and Ecclesiastes, we shouldn't interpret Proverbs as if it were making unwavering guarantees about the assured outcomes of your choices in every situation. As one specific example, consider Proverbs 22:6. When it says, "Train up a child in the way he should go: and when he is old, he will not depart from it" (KJV), don't take this cause-and-effect statement as an ironclad promise with no exceptions ever. Sometimes good parenting results in good kids, but not always. Sometimes, the best parents have the worst kids. The problem with the dependability of this verse isn't with God's Word; it's with this fallen world. In Proverbs certain stated results are generally true, but not always true.[20]

Also, when we don't enjoy the expected benefits of wise living, these disappointing outcomes remind us that God uses more than mere reward to shape our lives to be more like Christ. Our Father's aim for his children goes beyond helping them escape poverty or illness. The Lord may wield the tool of blessing with his right hand and suffering with his left, but for the Christian both become the Great Physician's scalpel removing evil and promoting holiness and love.

*****

When you read Proverbs, you are viewing reality through a God-given lens or worldview. For human beings, all of whom are born wrongly related to God, others, the world, and even themselves, the worldview of Proverbs throws open windows to see the way the universe truly is. But in the roughly 3,000 years since these proverbs were written, who has been able to fully absorb and apply its wisdom? How can someone possibly enter into a wise and proper relationship with God, his world, and its inhabitants?

The Climax of Proverbs

EXEMPLARY WISDOM

Every person who's ever lived knows something of the struggle that would be required for a consistent lifetime of wise thinking, wise living, and wise speaking. Ever since Adam and Eve rebelled against God (Genesis 3), no member of the human race has ever fully and rightly been related to God, others, this world, and his or her own person.

Except one. Jesus Christ personally embodied the fullest expression of wise living. Even as a child, he modeled true wisdom (Luke 2:40, 52), demonstrating proper priorities in the face of competing relationships (Luke 2:41–51). In his years of maturity and ministry, his actions continued to exude wisdom (Luke 11:29–32).

Jesus also wisely taught God's wisdom. When he spoke, people heard nothing less than the Father's own wisdom (cf. Luke 11:49; Matthew 23:34ff). His teaching, including his many parables (the Old Testament Hebrew word for "proverb" is commonly translated "parable" in the

Greek Old Testament), often resembles the wisdom literature of the Old Testament.[21] Jesus is the high-water mark of all such biblical wisdom (Matthew 11:13–19; 12:42). And all those who build their lives on his instruction, are found to be men and women of wisdom (Matthew 7:24ff). If ever someone fit the description, "Do good? Get good," it was Jesus. His wisdom-saturated life rightly earned life and blessing.

However, when you compare his life with his death, Jesus's crucifixion shouts the outrageous conclusion: "Do good? Get evil." Yet under the cloak of this seeming madness, Jesus's unjust death actually radiates God's brilliant wisdom (Romans 11:30). To all human appearances his death signified weakness, folly, and failure, but in actuality the cross of Christ was nothing less than "the power of God and the wisdom of God" in accomplishing God's plan of salvation graciously given to sinners (1 Corinthians 1:18–24).[22]

GENEROUS WISDOM

Everything Jesus did, he did in wisdom. Despite hardship, opposition, and betrayal during his life and ministry, Jesus always rightly related to God, others, the world, and himself. Therefore, he duly earned the reward of wise living: life and blessing (Proverbs 8:35). And this blessing does not just belong to him, but also to all those who are united to him by faith (Colossians 2:9–12). For all who are *in him*, Jesus Christ has become "to us wisdom from God" (1 Corinthians 1:30). That is, all Christians have now been decisively set into a right relationship with God, Christ having forever delivered them from the destroyer of that relationship: the penalty, the power, and (one day) even the presence of sin (1 Corinthians 1:30).[23]

This wisdom, which Christ has generously given to his people, entails that the blessing of God comes to us because of grace, not through our own efforts. Since no sinner could ever have lived in perfect wisdom, Christ's wisdom has now reversed the sequence of blessing for his people. In Christ, wisdom ultimately no longer follows the pattern: "Do good? Get good." For the believer, the order is now: "Get good? (from Christ) Do good" (for Christ).[24]

This means that as we are now rightly related to Christ (who is perfectly related to the Father), we too are enabled by the Holy Spirit to rightly relate to the Father, and through him, to everything and everyone else.[25] Through Christ and the Spirit, believers may now, more than ever, properly relate to God, other people, and this universe, even as we face difficulties and pain in this fallen world.[26]

Consequently, wise living should characterize the Christian's way (Colossians 4:5), for the storehouse of God's wisdom is located in the Lord Jesus Christ himself (Colossians 2:3). And from this bountiful treasury, believers may make regular, Spirit-enabled withdrawals as situations arise—both by asking for gifts of wisdom (James 1:5–6) and also by exercising God-given discernment of mind (2 Timothy 2:7; Ephesians 5:10).[27]

And while this God-given wisdom will often bring blessing from God, these rewards aren't our deepest motivation. Nor do the promises of blessing exempt Christians from suffering and sacrifice for others. If Jesus embodied wisdom and still embraced suffering in his life and death, should we expect any less? For the Christian, living in wisdom isn't just the better calculation, the smooth road to prosperity. The path of understanding may be lined with roses but always leads to a cross.

For at this place of death, true wisdom came to full bloom in the person of Christ. And because of his life and death, he stands as our ultimate Example and Source of wisdom. Jesus modeled perfect wisdom, rightly relating to God and everything else. And now he has graciously passed on to his people, that same wisdom.

Thus, as the believing men and women of one generation have generously received the wisdom from God, so they must preserve this treasure for the next generation—and pass it on.

✒ Proverbs One

Guided Tour

The first chapter begins by explaining the purpose of the entire book: to impart the wisdom (with its benefits) which springs from a healthy "fear of the LORD" (1:1–7). After this overarching introduction to the entire book, chapter 1 divides into two further sections: the first of many father-son talks (1:8–19); and the first place "Wisdom" actually speaks, as if a real person: Lady Wisdom (1:20–33). Here are some things to look for while you read. The first seven verses unpack the purpose of Proverbs in terms of what is learned (1:2–3), who may benefit (1:4–5), how it is communicated (1:6), and where to start (1:7). In 1:8–19, two opposing characters simultaneously demand your attention. To whose words will you listen—the wise words of a father or the foolish words of bad "friends"? Then in 1:20–33, wisdom, now personified as a Lady, calls out, summoning people to listen to her counsel. Notice the generous benefits awaiting those who listen to Lady Wisdom and the altogether different consequences for those who refuse her.

AT-A-GLANCE

1:1–7	The Purpose of Proverbs
1:8–19	Words of a Wise Father: Don't follow the crowd
1:20–33	The Invitation of Lady Wisdom

¹The proverbs of Solomon son of David, king of Israel:
² to know wisdom and instruction,
    to understand words of insight;
³ to accept instruction in prudent behavior,
    [to do] what is right, and just, and fair;
⁴ to give to the gullible shrewdness,
    to the young, knowledge and discretion—
⁵ let the wise hear and add to their learning,
    and let the insightful acquire guidance—

⁶ to understand a proverb, namely, a parable,
  the sayings of the wise, namely, their riddles.
⁷ The fear of the LORD is the beginning of knowledge,
  but fools despise wisdom and instruction.

⁸ Listen, my son, to your father's instruction,
  and do not let go of your mother's teaching,
⁹ for they are an attractive garland for your head,
  and a necklace for your throat.
¹⁰ My son, if sinful men tempt you, do not yield.
¹¹ If they say, "Come with us;
    let's set an ambush for blood,
    let's lie in wait for the innocent with no reason at all;
¹² let's swallow them alive, like Sheol,
    even whole, like those who go down to the Pit.
¹³ all kinds of precious wealth we will find,
    we will fill our houses with plunder;
¹⁴ cast lots with us, all of us will divide up one purse"—
¹⁵ do not go on the way with them,
    withhold your foot from their byway,
¹⁶ for their feet rush into evil,
    and they hasten to shed blood.
¹⁷ Surely a net is spread out in vain
    in the sight of any creature that flies,
¹⁸ but they set an ambush for their own blood;
    they lie in wait for their own lives.
¹⁹ Such are the paths of everyone who is greedy for gain;
    it takes away the life of the one who gets it.

²⁰ Wisdom cries aloud in the street,
    in the public squares she raises her voice;
²¹ on the highest walls she calls out,
    at the entrance of the gates to the city she makes her speech:
²² "How long, you gullible, will you love being gullible"—
    and mockers delight themselves with mocking,
    and fools hate knowledge?
²³ Turn back, [you gullible young people], to my rebuke;
    then I will pour forth my thoughts to you,
    I will make known to you my sayings.
²⁴ '[But] since I cry out, and you refuse [to listen],

and when I stretch out my hand, none gives heed,
  25 and you flout all my counsel,
  and to my rebuke you do not consent,
  26 I in turn will laugh when your disaster happens,
  I will scoff when your calamity comes—
  27 when your calamity comes like a storm,
  and like a whirlwind your disaster arrives,
  when distress and anguish come upon you.'
  28 Then they will call out to me, but I will not answer;
  they will look diligently for me but will not find me,
  29 because they hated knowledge,
  and the fear of the LORD they did not choose.
  30 They did not consent to my advice,
  they spurned my every rebuke,
  31 so they will eat from the fruit of their way,
  and from their schemes they will be filled.
  32 Surely the turning away of the gullible will kill them,
  and the complacency of fools will destroy them;
  33 but the one who obeys will dwell in security,
  even at ease, without fear of harm."

 Reflections

IDENTIFYING A VERSE

Write out the one verse that stood out to you from this chapter.

_____

_____

_____

Why did it stand out to you?

_____

_____

_____

GOING DEEPER

According to Proverbs 1:7; 29, and the comments from "A Bird's-Eye View" (page 9), how would you describe what it means for someone to live in the "fear of the LORD"?

_____

_____

_____

Over the course of your life, what person, thing, or experience (other than God) takes up most of your time, attention, and thoughts? (It may be what you most often think about, desire strongly, or fear to lose.)

_____

_____

_____

What kinds of foolish (according to Proverbs' definition of "the fool") and deceitful lies might this "person, thing, or experience" tempt you to believe was true?

_____

_____

_____

_____

In your experience, describe how these lies have affected you in your life? What has helped you to see them as lies?

_____

_____

_____

_____

CONNECTING THE GOSPEL

Read Proverbs 1:7. When our fear of the LORD and even our wisest decisions are inadequate and weak, how does Isaiah 11:1–3 provide assurance and comfort by pointing to Christ our substitute?

_____

_____

_____

_____

PERSONALIZING A PRAYER

Write out a prayer for yourself and for _____ (fill in the name of the journal's recipient), using Proverbs 1. If you would like, use the pattern below or simply reword verses in Proverbs 1 into a prayer of help and thankfulness to God.

> **The Person** (What do you learn about God in that chapter of Proverbs that helps shape your prayer? E.g., "Father, you are full of wisdom . . .")
> **The Petition** (Based on something from Proverbs, what is a prayer request you're making for the final owner of this journal?)
> **The Purpose** (Using some desirable outcome expressed in Proverbs, what are you hoping that your request may accomplish?)
> **The Plea** (All Christian prayer is offered "in Jesus' name": on the basis of Christ's merits, not our own.)[28]

_____

_____

_____

_____

_____

_____

SHARING YOUR STORY

Write out the most important piece of advice you have received in your life (see Proverbs 1:8).

_____

_____

_____

_____

_____

Who gave you that advice?

_____

_____

_____

_____

Why has it proved to be so important?

_____

_____

_____

_____

In what ways do you see _____ already living out the advice you just gave?

_____

_____

_____

_____

✎ Proverbs Two

Guided Tour

The next father-son talk fills this entire chapter (2:1–22). The first ten verses feature the main section of fatherly advice, followed by a two-part illustration of wisdom's benefits of deliverance (2:12–15; 2:16–19) and a concluding application (2:20–22). In 2:1–10, the father explains how to become a wise person. Notice the if/then statements that help outline the progression of moving from folly to wisdom. (See the "Pathway of Wisdom" section of the Introduction, for a more in-depth discussion and outline of 2:1–10.) Beginning in verse 11, the father shares the protecting benefits of having acquired true wisdom: deliverance from the deception of wayward men (2:12–15) and wayward women (2:16 –19). The conclusion (2:20–22) summarizes the two pathways which a person may take and their respective destinations.

AT-A-GLANCE

2:1–10	How to Become Wise
2:11–15	Benefits of Wisdom: Protection from Wayward Men
2:16–19	Benefits of Wisdom: Protection from Wayward Women
2:20-22	Conclusion: The Two Destinies

¹ My son, if you accept my words,
    and my commands you store up with you—
² by making your ear attentive to wisdom,
    you will apply your heart to understanding—
³ indeed, if to insight you call out,
    to understanding you raise your voice;
⁴ if you seek it as for silver,
    and as for hidden treasures you search for it,
⁵ then you will understand the fear of the LORD,
    and the knowledge of God you will find;

⁶ for the LORD gives wisdom,
   from his mouth come knowledge and understanding;
⁷ he holds success in store for the upright—
   he is a shield to those who walk in blamelessness
⁸ by guarding the paths of justice—
   and the way of his loyal ones he watches over;
⁹ then you will understand what is right, and just,
   and fair, every good track;
¹⁰ for wisdom will enter your heart,
   and knowledge will be pleasant to your appetite;

¹¹ shrewdness will watch over you,
   understanding will guard you;
¹² to deliver you from the way of the evil man,
   from the man who speaks perversions,
¹³ those who abandon straight paths
   to walk in ways of darkness;
¹⁴ those who are joyful in doing evil,
   [and] rejoice in evil perversions;
¹⁵ whose paths are crooked,
   and who are devious in their tracks;

¹⁶ to deliver you from the unchaste wife,
   from the outsider who causes her words to be smooth;
¹⁷ who abandons the companion of her youth,
   and forgets her covenant with God;
¹⁸ surely her byway leads down into death,
   and her tracks to the realm of the dead;
¹⁹ all who enter into her will not return,
   and they will not reach the paths of life;

²⁰ and so you will walk in the way of good people,
   and the paths of the righteous you will keep;
²¹ surely the upright will dwell in the land,
   and the blameless will be left in it;
²² but the wicked will be cut off from the earth,
   and the treacherous will be torn from it.

 Reflections

IDENTIFYING A VERSE

Write out the verse that stood out to you from this chapter.

_____

_____

_____

Why did it stand out to you?

_____

_____

_____

_____

GOING DEEPER

Reflect on Proverbs 2:6. In your own words, use this verse to explain to the future owner of this journal where wisdom is to be found.

_____

_____

_____

_____

According to Proverbs 2:1–11 and the comments in the Guided Tour, if children asks where they can hear the wisdom that comes from God himself, where might they find it?

_____

_____

_____

_____

Proverbs 2:1–4 describes the person who seeks wisdom. List the actions this person takes.

_____

_____

_____

_____

CONNECTING THE GOSPEL

Read Proverbs 2:3–4 and Colossians 2:1–3 (below). What comparisons and parallels would you draw between them? How do these verses direct your search for wisdom?

_____

_____

_____

_____

PERSONALIZING A PRAYER

Write out a prayer for yourself and for _____, using Proverbs 2 and Colossians 2:1–3. Ask that your heart and _____'s heart will be directed toward wisdom.

> For I want you to know how great a struggle I have for you and for those at Laodicea and for all who have not seen me face to face, that their hearts may be encouraged, being knit together in love, to reach all the riches of full assurance of understanding and the knowledge of God's mystery, which is Christ, in whom are hidden all the treasures of wisdom and knowledge. (Colossians 2:1–3)

_____

_____

_____

_____

_____

SHARING YOUR STORY

What is the most significant thing (that had the most impact on you and/or someone else) that you feel you've done in life? And describe your role in it.

_____

_____

_____

_____

Why was it so significant?

_____

_____

_____

_____

What kind of successes would you wish for the future owner of this journal? And why?

_____

_____

_____

_____

✒ Proverbs Three

Guided Tour

This chapter builds on the previous one. Chapter 2 taught about gaining wisdom (*acquisition*), while chapter 3 gives instruction about keeping it (*preservation*, see 3:1–2). The first half of this chapter divides into six two-verse blocks, each pair of verses containing a command and a reward. Broadly, there are rewards for continuing to live wisely toward people (3:3–4) and toward God—in trust (3:5–6), in humility (3:7–8), in worship (3:9–10), and in submission (3:11–12). In the last half of the chapter (3:13–35), a father wants his son to understand that persisting in wisdom will bring abundant benefits: to anyone in general (3:13–20) and for the reader in particular (3:21–26). Notice all the specific commands the father employs to describe what an ongoing lifestyle of wisdom toward people concretely looks like (3:27–31). And concluding the chapter, the father communicates not only the benefits for continuing in wisdom, but also the consequences for abandoning it (3:32–35).

AT-A-GLANCE

3:1–12	How to Protect the Wisdom You Have
3:13–35	How to Benefit from the Wisdom You've Protected

¹ My son, do not forget my teaching,
  and let your heart guard my commandments,
² for length of days and years of life,
  and peace and prosperity they will add to you.
³ Let kindness and faithfulness not leave you;
  bind them upon your neck,
⁴ and find favor and good repute
  in the eyes of God and humankind.
⁵ Trust in the LORD with all your heart,
  and on your own understanding do not rely;
⁶ in all your ways desire his presence,
  and he will make your paths straight and smooth.

⁷ Do not be wise in your own eyes;
  fear the Lᴏʀᴅ and shun evil;
⁸ let there be healing to your navel,
  and refreshment to your bones.
⁹ Honor the Lᴏʀᴅ from your wealth,
  from the firstfruits of all your produce,
¹⁰ and your granaries will be filled with plenty,
  and your vats will overflow with new wine.
¹¹ The discipline of the Lᴏʀᴅ, my son, do not reject,
  and do not loathe his correction,
¹² because whom the Lᴏʀᴅ loves he corrects,
  even as a father the son in whom he delights.

¹³ Blessed is the human being who finds wisdom,
  the human being who obtains understanding;
¹⁴ for the profit she give is better than the profit of silver,
  and her revenue than gold.
¹⁵ She is more precious than corals;
  all desirable things cannot compare with her.
¹⁶ long life is in her right hand;
  in her left, wealth and honor.
¹⁷ Her ways are pleasant ways,
  and all her byways are peace and prosperity.
¹⁸ She is a tree of life to those who take hold of her,
  and those who hold her fast are each declared blessed.
¹⁹ The Lᴏʀᴅ by wisdom founded the earth,
  established the heavens by understanding;
²⁰ by his knowledge the depths were split open
  and the clouds drip dew.
²¹ My son, let them [wisdom and understanding] not
  depart from your eyes,
  guard sound judgment and discretion,
²² so that they may become life for you,
  [and] an attractive ornament for your neck.
²³ Then you will walk securely in your way,
  and your foot will not stumble.
²⁴ When you lie down, you will not dread;
  and when you fall asleep, your sleep will be pleasing.
²⁵ Do not be afraid of sudden calamity,
  or the ruin of the wicked when it comes;

²⁶ for the LORD will be at your side
   and he will guard your foot from capture.
²⁷ Do not withhold [doing] good from those to whom it is due,
   when you have the power to do [good].
²⁸ Do not say to your neighbor, "Go and come back,
   and tomorrow I will give,"
   and all the while you have it with you.
²⁹ Do not plan evil against your neighbor,
   while he is dwelling trustingly with you.
³⁰ Do not bring an accusation against a person without reason,
   if he has not done you evil.
³¹ Do not envy a violent person,
   and do not choose any of his ways;
³² for the devious are an abomination to the LORD,
   but with the upright is his counsel.
³³ The LORD's curse is on the house of the wicked,
   but the abode of the righteous he blesses.
³⁴ If it is matter of mockers, he mocks;
   and if it is a matter of the humble and oppressed, he shows favor.
³⁵ The wise will inherit honor,
   but fools are those who acquire disgrace.

 ## Reflections

IDENTIFYING A VERSE

Write out the verse that stood out to you from this chapter.

_____

_____

_____

Why did it stand out to you?

_____

_____

_____

GOING DEEPER

According to Proverbs 3:5, what is the opposite of trusting in the LORD with all your heart?

_____

_____

_____

_____

Read Proverbs 3:7. What phrase in this verse parallels the answer you gave to the previous question?

_____

_____

_____

_____

Based on your previous answers, in your own words, what does the following phrase mean: "on your own understanding do not rely" (3:5)?

_____

_____

_____

_____

Over the years, how have you seen people follow their own version of wisdom, in opposition to God's wisdom? What were the results?

_____

_____

_____

_____

CONNECTING THE GOSPEL

Read Proverbs 3:1–4 and Luke 2:52. When you fail to live wisely, remember that Jesus (according to Luke 2:52), fulfilled this portion of God's Word, living the perfectly wise life in your place. In what ways did he embody the humility, generosity, and other virtues commended in Proverbs 3?

_____

_____

_____

_____

Right now, where in your life do you most need the wisdom that Jesus graciously models and gives?

_____

_____

_____

_____

Right now, where do you see _____ needing the same wisdom from Jesus?

_____

_____

_____

_____

PERSONALIZING A PRAYER

Write out a prayer using some portion of Proverbs 3. Ask God for the wisdom you and _____ need for each day. Be sure to include those specific areas that you would like to grow in wisdom and that you would like to see _____ grow.

_____

_____

_____

_____

SHARING YOUR STORY

Family is important for passing on wisdom (3:1, 11–12, 21, 33). Fill in
the family tree below.

Tell one story about someone in your family tree (for example: an unusual
job, a long trip, an immigrant from another country, a funny story, etc.)

_____

_____

_____

_____

Tell one story about what _____ did as a child that was funny or
memorable or unusual.

_____

_____

_____

✒ Proverbs Four

Guided Tour

This chapter contains three more father-son talks: 4:1–9; 4:10–19; and 4:20–27. Each section begins with a father addressing "my son" or "my sons," and each highlights the value of wisdom. In 4:1–9, a father not only tells his sons to get wisdom, he also explains where he himself had found wisdom: from his own father. This multi-generational wisdom has stood the test of time, proven itself to be sound and reliable (4:2), and should, therefore, be confidently taken to heart (4:4–5). In this way, the benefits of such tried-and-true wisdom endure through multiple generations. In the next section (4:10–19), the father then illustrates the value of wise living by using the imagery of someone walking on a path. The instruction? Walk straight on the path of wisdom always. Notice what happens if someone were to leave this path (4:12, 16, 19). In the final section (4:20–27), the picture changes from a path to a person. Take note of how many different parts of the human body should be somehow related to wisdom. Wisdom isn't merely a pursuit for all of life, but for all of you.

AT-A-GLANCE

4:1–9	The Value of Wisdom through the Generations
4:10–19	The Value of Wisdom on the Road of Life
4:20–27	The Value of Wisdom for All of Life

¹ Listen, sons, to a father's instruction,
  and pay attention to knowledge that gives insight.
² Because I give to you a good education,
  do not leave my teaching.
³ When I was a son to my father,
  still tender, and cherished by my mother,
⁴ then he taught me, and he said to me,
  "Let your heart take hold of my words,
  keep my commands and live.

⁵ Get wisdom! Get insight!
  Do not forget and do not turn aside
  from the words of my mouth!
⁶ Do not leave her, and she will keep you;
  love her, and she will guard you.
⁷ The beginning of wisdom is [this], get wisdom!
  In exchange for all your acquisitions, get insight.
⁸ Cherish her, and she will exalt you;
  she will honor you if you embrace her.
⁹ She will bestow a garland to grace your head;
  a splendid crown she will give you."

¹⁰ Listen, my son, and accept my words,
  that the years of life may be many for you.
¹¹ I instruct you in the way of wisdom,
  I lead you along straight tracks.
¹² When you walk, your step will not be hampered;
  and if you run, you will not stumble.
¹³ Hold on to instruction; do not stop;
  guard it, for it is your life.
¹⁴ Do not enter the path of the wicked
  and do not take strides in the way of evil men.
¹⁵ Flout it; do not travel on it;
  turn aside from going upon it, and pass on.
¹⁶ For they are robbed of sleep till they forge evil;
  and their sleep is torn away unless they make [somebody] stumble.
¹⁷ For they eat the bread of wickedness,
  and the wine of violent acts they drink.
¹⁸ Now the path of the righteous is like the morning sun,
  shining ever brighter until the day is firm.
¹⁹ The way of the wicked is like darkness;
  they do not know what trips them up.

²⁰ My son, pay attention to my words;
  turn your ear to my sayings.
²¹ Do not allow them to depart from before your eyes;
  keep them within your heart;
²² for they are life to those who find them,
  and a remedy for one's whole body.
²³ Above every watch, guard your heart,

for everything you do flows from it.
²⁴ Keep a crooked mouth away from you,
   and devious lips put far away from you.
²⁵ Let your eyes look straight ahead,
   and let your pupils look straight in front of you.
²⁶ Watch the track for your foot,
   and let all your ways be steadfast.
²⁷ Do not turn to the right or to the left;
   keep your foot from evil.

 ## Reflections

IDENTIFYING A VERSE

Write out the verse that stood out to you from this chapter.

_____

_____

_____

Why did it stand out to you?

_____

_____

_____

_____

GOING DEEPER

Use Proverbs 4:4–9 to list every action that you should take toward wisdom (or its synonyms: words, commands, understanding, etc.).

_____

_____

_____

How would you summarize these into two or three action steps for the journal's future owner to pursue?

_____

_____

_____

_____

Read Proverbs 4:10–19. What are all the benefits of wisdom (in contrast to the destruction of folly)?

_____

_____

_____

_____

How might these benefits encourage _____ to take the action steps you identified in 4:4–9?

_____

_____

_____

_____

CONNECTING THE GOSPEL

Read Proverbs 4:23 and James 3:13–18. How does James 3:13–18 describe the fruit that grows from a wise person's heart?

_____

_____

_____

What actions and attitudes indicate the presence of folly in the heart (Mark 7:20–23)?

_____

_____

_____

_____

How do you handle it when you notice folly in your life? How would you recommend _____ handles it when he/she notices folly in his/her life? (See 1 John 1:8–9 below.)

_____

_____

_____

_____

PERSONALIZING A PRAYER

Write out a prayer for yourself and _____ using some portion of Proverbs 4 and 1 John 1:8–9:

> If we say we have no sin, we deceive ourselves, and the truth is not in us. If we confess our sins, he is faithful and just to forgive us our sins and to cleanse us from all unrighteousness. (1 John 1:8–9)

As part of your prayer, give thanks to God for Jesus who purchased our forgiveness with his life.

_____

_____

_____

_____

SHARING YOUR STORY

Since Proverbs 4 highlights the wisdom passed along from one generation to the next, what life lessons do you remember being taught as a child by someone who was caring for you?

_____

_____

_____

_____

What life lesson would you want the recipient of this journal to remember and be sure to pass along to his or her own children?

_____

_____

_____

_____

✒ Proverbs Five

Guided Tour

This entire chapter (5:1–23) features the next father-son talk; this time it's about sexual faithfulness. And the battle for purity begins with a war of words (5:1–14). The issue is: Which words will you heed? A wise father speaks words of instruction (5:1, 7, 12–13), while the wayward woman also speaks competing words of temptation which bring impending destruction (5:3ff). You can read the actual content of the father's words of instruction in the main body of the chapter (5:7–23). In this section, he guides toward purity by giving three commands to be obeyed (5:8, 15, 17). He motivates toward purity by describing the negative consequences of sexual indulgence outside of marriage (5:9–14) and by extolling the positive delights of sexual love inside of marriage (5:15–19). And in the final four verses, the father provides the basis for the chapter's instructions: the Lord himself. Throughout the entire chapter, notice how the father does more than merely command and warn; he also reasons with his son. He provides rationale for pursuing purity. Look for verses where you are called to consider and think for yourself about the rewards of purity and the ruin of sin.

AT-A-GLANCE

5:1–6	The Battle for Purity: Give Attention to Wisdom
5:7–14	The Battle for Purity: Command #1 and Consequences
5:15–16	The Battle for Purity: Command #2 and Consequences
5:17–19	The Battle for Purity: Command #3 and Consequences
5:20–23	The Battle for Purity: Compelling Reasons

¹ My son, pay attention to my wisdom;
  turn your ear to my words of understanding,
² that you may keep discretion,
  and that your lips may guard knowledge.

³ For the lips of the unchaste wife drip honey,
   and her palate is smoother than oil.
⁴ But in the end she is bitter, like wormwood;
   sharp, like a double-edged sword.
⁵ Her feet are going down to death,
   her steps lay hold of the grave.
⁶ The path of life she does not watch;
   her tracks meander aimlessly; she does not know it.

⁷ So now, sons, listen to me,
   and do not turn aside from the words of my mouth.
⁸ Keep your way far from her,
   and do not draw near to the door of her house,
⁹ lest you give your splendor to others,
   and your dignity to the cruel;
¹⁰ lest strangers be filled with your strength,
   and your strenuous labors will be in an outsider's house.
¹¹ And you will groan at the end of your life,
   when your body and your flesh are spent;
¹² and you will say, "How I hated instruction,
   [how] my heart spurned rebuke.
¹³ And I did not listen to the voice of my teachers,
   I did not turn my ear to those who taught me.
¹⁴ I was soon in serious trouble
   in the midst of the congregation and the assembly."

¹⁵ Drink water from your own cistern,
   and flowing streams from the midst of your own well.
¹⁶ Should your springs overflow without?
   Your channels of water in the open squares?

¹⁷ Let them be for yourself alone,
   and have no strangers with you.
¹⁸ May your wellspring be blessed,
   and get pleasure from the wife of your youth.
¹⁹ [May she be] a lovingmaking doe, a graceful mountain goat;
   may her breasts drench you at all times;
   and with her caresses may you always become intoxicated.

²⁰ Now why be intoxicated, my son, with an unchaste wife?
   [Why] embrace the bosom of an unfaithful woman?

²¹ For a man's ways are before the eyes of the Lord;
   he is watching all his tracks.
²² His inquities will catch him;
   and with the cords of his sin he will be held fast.
²³ He will die in his lack of instruction,
   and in the abundance of his folly he will be led astray.

Reflections

IDENTIFYING A VERSE

Write out the verse that stood out to you from this chapter.

_____

_____

_____

Why did it stand out to you?

_____

_____

_____

_____

GOING DEEPER

In Proverbs 5:8, 15, 17, what three commands does Solomon give, related to sexual integrity? (Notice how these commands fall into two categories: sin that is forbidden and pleasure that is encouraged.)

_____

_____

_____

_____

In your own words, summarize these commands for the benefit of the person who will receive this journal.

_____

_____

_____

_____

Read Proverbs 5:21 and paraphrase this verse in your own words.

_____

_____

_____

_____

The person to whom you plan to give this journal will face sexual temptation at some time in life. What encouragements, reminders, and/or warnings would you give them, based on 5:20–23?

_____

_____

_____

_____

CONNECTING THE GOSPEL

Read Proverbs 5:8 and 2 Timothy 2:22. What additional insights does 2 Timothy 2:22 provide on this verse?

_____

_____

_____

Read Ephesians 5:31–32. How does Jesus set the ultimate example of faithfulness to his bride?

_____

_____

_____

What do you think will help you and _____ live with purity and faithfulness in your respective relationships?

_____

_____

_____

PERSONALIZING A PRAYER

Write out a prayer for yourself and _____ using some portion of Proverbs 5. Also use Ephesians 5:25 in your prayer, asking to grow to be more like Jesus who gave his life for you.

> Husbands, love your wives, as Christ loved the church and gave himself up for her. (Ephesians 5:25)

_____

_____

_____

_____

SHARING YOUR STORY

If you are married, share the story about how you met your wife/husband. Or share the story of how your parents (or grandparents met).

_____

_____

_____

_____

Describe a marriage that has inspired you with the way the husband and wife have loved each other (this could be your marriage or the marriage of someone you know).

_____

_____

_____

_____

✒ Proverbs Six

Guided Tour

The now familiar words, "my son," begin each half of this chapter (6:1 and 6:20), both of which overflow with striking imagery and analogies. The first half (6:1–19) contains three separate sections, each issuing a warning (6:1–5, 6–11, 12–19). Section 1 warns, "Don't become a prisoner" through financial entanglements (6:1–5). Section 2 warns, "Don't become a victim" to laziness and its consequences (6:6–11). Section 3 warns, "Don't become a target" of those in authority by plotting treacherously against them (6:12–19). In summary: Live wisely in order to stay free, safe, and secure. The second half of the chapter (6:20–35) closely resembles the discussion of sexual faithfulness in Proverbs 5. Notice the same opening "war of words" (6:20–24), the main command to be pure (6:25), the use of rationale in the pursuit of purity (6:27–28, 30–35), and the many awful consequences of sexual sin vividly pictured throughout.

AT-A-GLANCE

6:1–5	Warning 1: Don't become a prisoner to money
6:6–11	Warning 2: Don't become a victim to laziness
6:12–19	Warning 3: Don't become a target through stirring conflict
6:20–35	The Price of Purity: Commands and Reasons

¹ My son, if you have become surety for your neighbor,
   [if] you have struck your palm for a stranger,
² you have been ensnared by the words of your lips;
   you have been captured by the words of your mouth.
³ So do this, my son, and deliver yourself,
   for you have come into the hand of your neighbor:
   go, weary yourself and badger your neighbors.
⁴ Do not give sleep to your eyes,
   nor slumber to your pupils.

⁵ Deliver yourself as a gazelle from someone's hand,
   and as a bird from the hand of the fowler.

⁶ Go to the ant, you sluggard;
   observe its ways and become wise.
⁷ It has no overseer,
   officer, or ruler.
⁸ It provides for its grain in summer;
   it gathers in its food in the harvest.
⁹ How long, you sluggard, will you keep lying down?
   When will you rise from your sleep?
¹⁰ A little sleep, a little slumber,
   a little folding of the arms to lie down,
¹¹ and your poverty will come upon you like a vagrant,
   your scarcity, like an armed man.

¹² An insurrectionist, a malevolent person,
   is one who goes with a crooked mouth,
¹³ maliciously winks his eyes, shuffles his feet,
   and points with his fingers.
¹⁴ Perversions are in his heart; he plans evil at all times.
   He unleashes conflicts.
¹⁵ Therefore, suddenly his calamity will come;
   in an instant he will be broken, and without a remedy.
¹⁶ They are six [abominations] the LORD hates,
   yea, [they are] seven abominations to him:
¹⁷ haughty eyes, a lying tongue,
   and hands that shed innocent blood,
¹⁸ a heart that plans malevolent schemes,
   feet that hasten to run to evil,
¹⁹ a lying witness, a perjurer,
   and one who unleashes conflicts among relatives.

²⁰ Guard, my son, your father's commandment,
   and do not let go of your mother's teaching.
²¹ Bind them regularly upon your heart,
   fasten them upon your throat.
²² When you walk, she will lead you;
   when you lie down, she will guard you.
   Then you will awake, (and) she will speak to you.

²³ For the commandment is a lamp, and the teaching is a light,
and the corrections of instruction are the way of life;
²⁴ to guard you from your neighbor's wife,
from the smoothness of the unfaithful wife's tongue.
²⁵ Do not covet her beauty in your heart,
and do not let her capture you with the pupils of her eyes;
²⁶ for the price of a prostitute can be reduced to a loaf of bread,
but the wife of a man hunts for precious life.
²⁷ Can a man carry fire in his bosom
and his clothes not be burned?
²⁸ Or can a man walk about on glowing coals
and his feet not be branded?
²⁹ So is the one who enters into his neighbor's wife;
all who touch her will not escape punishment.
³⁰ People do not show contempt for a thief if he steals
to satisfy his appetite when he is hungry;
³¹ but if he is caught, he must repay sevenfold;
all the wealth of his household he will give.
³² The adulterer is one who lacks sense;
as for one who ruins his own life, he does it.
³³ He will find strokes and shame,
and his reproach will not be wiped away.
³⁴ For jealousy [arouses] the wrath of a man,
and he will not show compassion when he exacts revenge.
³⁵ He will not accept any compensation,
and he will not yield though you enlarge the bribe.

 Reflections

IDENTIFYING A VERSE

Write out the verse that stood out to you from this chapter.

_____

_____

_____

Why did it stand out to you?

_____

_____

_____

GOING DEEPER

In your own words, summarize the individual messages of 6:1–5; 6:6–11; and 6:12–19, addressing your words directly to this journal's future owner (e.g., "Remember, _____, that . . .").

6:1–5 _____

_____

_____

_____

6:6–11 _____

_____

_____

_____

6:12–19 _____

_____

_____

_____

CONNECTING THE GOSPEL

Read Proverbs 6:12–19 and Matthew 5:9. When we seek to live as true peacemakers (not one who "unleashes conflict"), what kind of actions and attitudes will most reflect our heavenly Father (Matthew 5:9)?

"Blessed are the peacemakers, for they shall be called sons of God."
(Matthew 5:9)

_____

_____

_____

What additional insight or direction does 2 Corinthians 5:18–20 give
for being a peacemaker?

_____

_____

_____

PERSONALIZING A PRAYER

Before you pray, think about what ultimate reward Jesus promises to
those who pursue purity of heart (Matthew 5:8, below). Write out a
prayer for yourself and _____ using some part of Proverbs 6. Also
use Matthew 5:8 as you pray for yourself and _____—that you
will want a heart that pursues purity because of an even greater desire
to know God.

_____

_____

_____

"Blessed are the pure in heart, for they shall see God." (Matthew
5:8)

_____

_____

_____

_____

SHARING YOUR STORY

Proverbs 6:1–19 describes various everyday activities. What does a regular day for you look like? (When do you get up, what do you do, what are your routines on a normal day?)

_____

_____

_____

_____

How is this different than when you were in your twenties? Thirties? Or other seasons of life?

_____

_____

_____

_____

What life habits have you found that serve you well as part of your regular routines?

_____

_____

_____

_____

How did you learn this habit or practice?

_____

_____

_____

_____

✒ Proverbs Seven

Guided Tour

The main section of this chapter (7:6–23) sits between two bookends: a positive introduction (7:1–5) and a negative conclusion (7:24–27), both of which begin with "my son" or "my sons." The introduction and conclusion also feature the commands to "listen" or "pay attention" to the father's words, which stand in contrast to the seducing words of the wicked woman (7:14–20). As in chapter 5, purity doesn't begin with protecting your eyes, but with guarding your ears. In the main middle section (7:6–23), the father imparts godly wisdom about human sexuality, not by giving more commands or rationale, but this time by dramatically sketching a real-life scenario. By mentally picturing this imaginary situation, you, the reader, are helped to internalize wise strategies for pursuing purity, even as you virtually observe and feel the temptation and destruction of sexual sin.

AT-A-GLANCE

7:1–5	Positive Introduction: Listen to Wisdom and Find Protection
7:6–23	Scenario: Dangers of Sexual Sin
7:24–27	Negative Conclusion: Listen to Wisdom and Avoid Destruction

¹ My son, keep my sayings,
  and my commands store up with you;
² keep my commands and live,
  and my teaching as the apple of your eye;
³ bind them upon your fingers;
  write them on the tablet of your heart;
⁴ say to wisdom, "You are my sister,"
  and call out to insight, "You are my relative";
⁵ to keep you from the unfaithful wife,
  from the unchaste wife who causes her words to be smooth.

⁶ For standing at the window of my house,
  through the opening I looked down.
⁷ And I saw among the gullible,
  I gave heed among the sons to a youth who lacked sense.
⁸ He was passing through the street beside her corner;
  he was taking strides on the way to her house,
⁹ at dusk, in the evening of the day,
  with the approach of night and darkness.
¹⁰ And look! a woman comes out to face him
  in the garb of a harlot and with a cunning heart.
¹¹ She is unruly and defiant;
  her feet do not settle down in her house;
¹² now in the street, now in the squares,
  and beside every corner she lies in wait.
¹³ And she grabbed him and kissed him;
  she hardened her face and said to him:
¹⁴ "I owed a fellowship sacrifice;
  today I fulfilled my vows.
¹⁵ Therefore, I came out to face you,
  to seek your face diligently, and I found you!
¹⁶ I have provided my couch with coverlets,
  embroidered stuff, the linen of Egypt.
¹⁷ I have perfumed my bed
  with myrrh, lign-aloes, and cinnamon.
¹⁸ Come, let us drink our fill with making love until morning;
  let us enjoy each other with love;
¹⁹ for my husband is not at home;
  he went on a distant journey.
²⁰ He took in his hand a purse filled with silver;
  he will come home at full moon.
²¹ She turned him aside with her immense persuasiveness;
  with the blandishments of her lips she routed him.
²² He went after her suddenly,
  as an ox enters a slaughterhouse,
  and as a stag stepping into a noose
²³ until an arrow splits open his liver;
  as a bird hastens into a trap.
  And he does not know [he acts] against his own life.

²⁴ So now, sons, listen to me;
    pay attention to the words of my mouth.
²⁵ Do not let your heart turn aside into her ways;
    do not go astray into her paths.
²⁶ For she has toppled many slain [victims],
    even the powerful, all those killed by her.
²⁷ Her house presents the ways to the grave,
    descending to the chambers of death.

Reflections

IDENTIFYING A VERSE

Write out the verse that stood out to you from this chapter.

_____

_____

_____

Why did it stand out to you?

_____

_____

_____

GOING DEEPER

In Proverbs 7:5, 21, what turns the young man's heart toward the adulterous woman?

_____

_____

_____

_____

In contrast to the previous answer, what do 7:1–4, 24 say is essential in order to protect the young man from the adulterous woman?

_____

_____

_____

_____

Put these verses in your own words, and direct them to the person who will own this journal.

_____

_____

_____

_____

CONNECTING THE GOSPEL

Read Proverbs 7:3 and 2 Corinthians 3:3 (below). Proverbs 7 asks the reader to listen to God's Word. What tends to keep you from the kind of heart-level listening to God's Word that would change you?

_____

_____

_____

_____

What is needed, according to 2 Corinthians 3:3, for believers to have the truth of God written deep within their hearts?

_____

_____

_____

How might Luke 11:13 inform your and _____'s next steps toward a heart-level listening to God's truth?

> "If you then, who are evil, know how to give good gifts to your children, how much more will the heavenly Father give the Holy Spirit to those who ask him!" (Luke 11:13)

_____

_____

_____

_____

PERSONALIZING A PRAYER

Write out a prayer for yourself and _____ reflecting some portion of Proverbs 7. Also use Luke 11:13 and 2 Corinthians 3:3 as you pray for yourself and _____ that you both would have the Spirit of Christ write his word on your hearts.

> And you show that you are a letter from Christ delivered by us, written not with ink but with the Spirit of the living God, not on tablets of stone but on tablets of human hearts. (2 Corinthians 3:3)

_____

_____

_____

_____

SHARING YOUR STORY

Proverbs 7 pivots on the question: By whom are you being influenced? What three people influenced or motivated you the most as you were growing up?

_____

_____

_____

_____

Describe what they did and how it impacted you.

_____

_____

_____

_____

What advice would you give your twenty-year-old self?

_____

_____

_____

_____

✒ Proverbs Eight

Guided Tour

In chapter 1 wisdom, personified as a lady, scolded the foolish person (negatively) for ignoring her. Yet in this chapter, Lady Wisdom commends herself to the wise person (positively). In the five sections comprising chapter 8, Lady Wisdom commends her virtues, in hopes that everyone will seek and gain such excellent wisdom. The first section (8:1–5) issues her invitation—she is accessible to all who seek her, even to the naïve and foolish. The second section (8:6–9) announces Wisdom's reliability—she only speaks words that are true and right. This alignment of wisdom with truth finds amplification in 8:12–16, as it is applied there to rulers specifically. The third section (8:10–11) extols Wisdom's value—she is a treasure worth more than silver or gold. This wealth that wisdom gives receives amplification in 8:17–21, as it benefits all who love Wisdom. The fourth section (8:22–31) presents the credentials of Lady Wisdom. Her wisdom is superior and uncorrupted by this fallen world because she is better than the created order (8:22–26) and she is in sync with it (8:27–31). The fifth section (8:32–36) broadcasts Wisdom's summons to learn and live according to her ways, to walk the path of blessing.

AT-A-GLANCE

8:1–5	Wisdom's Invitation
8:6–9	Wisdom's Reliability—Part 1
8:10–11	Wisdom's Value—Part 1
8:12–16	Wisdom's Reliability—Part 2
8:17–21	Wisdom's Value—Part 2
8:22–31	Wisdom's Credentials
8:32–36	Wisdom's Summons

[1] Does not Wisdom call out,
  and Understanding raise her voice?

61

² On the highest points beside the way,
  at the crossroads she takes her stand.
³ Beside the gates, at the entries of the city,
  at the entrances of the openings she cries aloud:
⁴ "To you, men, I call out;
  indeed, I cry aloud [to you], humanity.
⁵ You gullible, understand shrewdness,
  and you fools, set your hearts on it.

⁶ Listen, because I speak what is right,
  and the opening of my lips speaks what is upright.
⁷ Surely my palate utters truth,
  and wickedness is an abomination to my lips.
⁸ All the words of my mouth are spoken in righteousness,
  and there is not one among them that is deceitful or perverse.
⁹ All of them are straight to those who understand,
  yes, upright to those who have found knowledge.

¹⁰ Choose my instruction instead of silver,
  my knowledge rather than choice gold,
¹¹ because wisdom is better than corals,
  and all the things one desires do not compare with her.

¹² I, Wisdom, dwell with shrewdness;
  and knowledge and discretion I find.
¹³ The fear of the LORD is hating evil—
  pride and arrogance and an evil way,
  and a perverse mouth I hate.
¹⁴ Counsel and resourcefulness belong to me;
  I am insight; heroic strength is mine.
¹⁵ Through me kings reign,
  and potentates decree what is right.
¹⁶ Through me rulers govern,
  and nobles—all the judges of the earth.

¹⁷ As for me, those who love me I love,
  and those who seek me diligently will find me.
¹⁸ Riches and honor are with me,
  enduring wealth and prosperity.
¹⁹ My fruit is better than gold, even pure gold,

and my yield than choice silver.
[20] I walk about in the path of righteousness,
   in the midst of the byways of justice,
[21] so that I bequeath property to those who love me,
   and I fill their treasuries.

[22] The LORD brought me forth as the first of his way,
   the earliest of his deeds from of old.
[23] In the most remote time I was formed,
   at the beginning, from the earliest times of the earth.
[24] When there were no depths I was brought forth,
   when there were no fountains abounding with water.
[25] Before the mountains had been planted,
   before the heights, I was brought forth.
[26] Before he made the earth and the open fields,
   and the world's first clods of dirt—
[27] When he fixed the heavens I was there,
   when he inscribed a circle on the face of the deep.
[28] When he made the clouds firm above,
   when he fixed fast the fountains of the deep;
[29] when he set for the sea its limits—
   and the waters can not go beyond his command—
   when he marked out the foundations of the earth.
[30] And I was beside him constantly;
   and I was delighting [before him] day after day,
   celebrating before him at all times;
[31] celebrating his inhabited earth,
   and my delight was humanity.

[32] So now, sons, listen to me—
   and blessed are those who keep my ways.
[33] Listen to instruction and become wise,
   and do not flout it.
[34] Blessed is the person who listens to me,
   keeping vigil at my doors day by day,
   observing the doorposts of my doorways;
[35] for the one who finds me finds life,
   and so obtains favor from the LORD,
[36] but the one who misses me is one who does violence against himself;
   all who hate me love death.

 Reflections

IDENTIFYING A VERSE

Write out the verse that stood out to you from this chapter.

_____

_____

_____

Why did it stand out to you?

_____

_____

_____

_____

GOING DEEPER

Although children may often think the wisdom of their parents is out of step with real life, what does 8:27–31 say about wisdom's actual relationship to the world we live in?

_____

_____

_____

In your own words (and with _____ in mind), list all the benefits of getting wisdom which are mentioned in 8:32–36.

_____

_____

_____

Proverbs 8:34 encourages us to seek God's wisdom on a daily basis. What advice or examples from your own life can you share with _____ about how God has helped you to do this?

_____

_____

_____

CONNECTING THE GOSPEL

Read Proverbs 8:17. The promise here is that those who seek God will find him. Finding God means finding wisdom. Psalm 105:3–4 (below) echoes this thought. According to James 1:5–6, what action must always accompany our quests for gaining wisdom from its Source?

_____

_____

_____

PERSONALIZING A PRAYER

Write out a prayer for yourself and _____ using Proverbs 8. Also use Psalm 105:3–4 as you pray for yourself and _____ that you both would seek the Lord and find all wisdom (along with joy and strength) in him.

> Glory in his holy name;
> let the hearts of those who seek the LORD rejoice!
> Seek the LORD and his strength;
> seek his presence continually! (Psalm 105:3–4)

_____

_____

_____

_____

SHARING YOUR STORY

Proverbs 8 emphasizes listening to the right kind of advice. What sayings (wise or otherwise) do you remember being used often by your family when you were growing up?

_____

_____

_____

_____

What did they mean?

_____

_____

_____

_____

Are there any particular stories attached to those sayings?

_____

_____

_____

_____

Have you repeated any of these sayings to the recipient of this journal? Which ones? And when?

_____

_____

_____

_____

✒ Proverbs Nine

Guided Tour

In this climactic conclusion to chapters 1–9, Lady Wisdom is again featured at the beginning of this chapter (9:1–6), joined by personified Folly at the end (9:13–18). Notice the comparison and contrast between them. Both Wisdom and Folly, having prepared rival feasts, invite all people to sit down at their respective tables and eat (9:4–6; 9:15–17). Both offer "free food" to the simple (9:4–6; 9:16–17). Yet in stark contrast, Wisdom's invitations are deliberate and loving (9:2–4), while Folly's are deceptive and lazy (9:14–15, 17). Between these two banquets lies the guest list (9:7–12): the two kinds of people receiving invitations to Wisdom's feast. On the one hand, some people, who live in the reality of God ("the fear the LORD," v.10), show signs of wisdom and respond positively to the invitation to grow in wisdom. On the other hand, stubbornly foolish people ("a mocker," vv. 7–8, 12) will despise invitations to Wisdom's feast (9:7–9). Each invitee will eat the fruit of his or her decision (9:11–12).

AT-A-GLANCE

9:1–6	The Superior Invitation to Wisdom's Feast
9:7–12	The People Receiving Invitations to the Feasts
9:13–18	The Inferior Invitation to Folly's Feast

¹ Wisdom has built her house;
  she has erected its seven pillars.
² She has slaughtered her animals; she has mixed her wine;
  and she has prepared her table.
³ She has sent out her servant girls; she cries out
  on the tops of the heights of the city,
⁴ "Whoever is gullible, let him turn aside here."
  As for the one who has no sense, she says to him,
⁵ "Come, dine on my food,
  and drink the wine I have mixed.

⁶ Leave your ways, you gullible ones, and live,
  and proceed on the way of insight."

⁷ Whoever chastises a mocker gets shame,
  and whoever corrects a wicked person gets hurt.
⁸ Do not correct a mocker lest he hate you;
  correct a wise person so that he will love you.
⁹ Give [instruction] to the wise so that he may become wiser still,
  inform the righteous so that he might increase learning.
¹⁰ The fear of the Lord is the beginning of wisdom,
  and knowledge of the Holy One is insight.
¹¹ Surely through wisdom your days will be many,
  and years of life will be added to you.
¹² If you are wise, you are wise for yourself;
  but [if] you mock, you alone will incur guilt.

¹³ The woman Folly is turbulent;
  she is totally gullible and does not know anything.
¹⁴ And she sits at the opening of her house,
  on a throne on the heights of the city,
¹⁵ calling out to those who pass along the way,
  to those who make their paths straight,
¹⁶ "Whoever is gullible, let him turn aside here."
  As for the one who has no sense, she says to him,
¹⁷ "Stolen water is sweet,
  and hidden food is pleasant."
¹⁸ But he does not know that the dead are there;
  those she invited are in the depths of the grave.

 Reflections

IDENTIFYING A VERSE

Write out the verse that stood out to you from this chapter.

_____

_____

_____

Why did it stand out to you?

_____

_____

_____

_____

GOING DEEPER

Read Proverbs 9:7–9 and the section describing the "mocker" (or "scoffer") in "A Bird's-Eye View of Proverbs" (page 12). In your own words, describe how and why this kind of person has gone wrong.

_____

_____

_____

Read Proverbs 9:10 and the section about "God" in "A Bird's-Eye View of Proverbs" (page 9). How would you explain the importance of living in the fear of the LORD to the person who will receive this journal?

_____

_____

_____

Give an example from your own life of how the reality of God (his holiness, love, mercy, grace, etc.) kept your life on the right path (or perhaps brought you back to it)?

_____

_____

_____

_____

CONNECTING THE GOSPEL

Read Proverbs 9:4. How does Jesus embody the gracious generosity of Lady Wisdom in the following passages?

Matthew 9:10–13 _____

_____

Matthew 11:28–30 _____

_____

Luke 7:34–35 _____

_____

Luke 14:15–24 _____

_____

PERSONALIZING A PRAYER

Write out a prayer for yourself and _____ using Proverbs 9. Using James 3:13–18, ask the Lord to give you and _____ a generous and wise heart.

> Who is wise and understanding among you? By his good conduct let him show his works in the meekness of wisdom. But if you have bitter jealousy and selfish ambition in your hearts, do not boast and be false to the truth. This is not the wisdom that comes down from above, but is earthly, unspiritual, demonic. For where jealousy and selfish ambition exist, there will be disorder and every vile practice. But the wisdom from above is first pure, then peaceable, gentle, open to reason, full of mercy and good fruits, impartial and sincere. And a harvest of righteousness is sown in peace by those who make peace. (James 3:13–18)

_____

_____

_____

_____

_____

SHARING YOUR STORY

Wisdom often brings the advantages that accompany a long life (9:11).
What about your life stands out in your memories from childhood? From
teenage years? From your twenties? Your thirties or later?

_____

_____

_____

_____

_____

_____

What are some of your favorite memories from when this journal's recipient was younger—from preschool and elementary ages? From middle
and high school? From college years?

_____

_____

_____

_____

_____

_____

_____

_____

Proverbs Ten

Guided Tour

This chapter begins the second main section of the book of Proverbs (chapters 10–31), and continues to remind readers of wisdom's value, a familiar theme from chapters 1–9 (cf. 1:8; 6:20). Yet this new section also introduces a new emphasis—the importance of not only living wisely, but living righteously. A truly wise person is also righteous (for more information on this topic, see "A Bird's-Eye View of Proverbs, pages 12–13). In harmony with the previous nine chapters, Proverbs 10 also regularly contrasts the difference between the wise way and the foolish way. In this chapter, look for the repeated use of the word "but," which signals a point of contrast. (This "antithetical" or "opposing" parallelism occurs frequently throughout chapters 10–15; see endnote 4 for more information.) Finally, chapter 10 may be divided into two halves: 10:1–16 and 10:17–32. In the first part, look for its two main themes: words and wealth, the mouth and money. The theme of speech also reappears occasionally in the second part of the chapter (10:17–32). While reading this second half, pay attention to what Solomon says about the positive results of wise living and the negative consequences of foolish living.

AT-A-GLANCE

10:1–16	Focus on Words and Wealth
10:17–32	Focus on Words and Consequences

¹ The proverbs of Solomon:
  A wise son makes his father glad,
    but a foolish son brings grief to his mother.
² Treasures gained by wickedness are of no eternal value,
    but righteousness delivers from death.
³ The LORD does not let the appetite of the righteous go unsatisfied,
    but what the wicked crave he thrusts aside.
⁴ A poor person is made with a slack palm,
    but the hand of diligent people brings wealth.

⁵ He who gathers [his food] in summer is a prudent son;
  he who sleeps in harvest is a shameful son.
⁶ Blessings come to the head of the righteous,
  but violence overwhelms the mouth of the wicked.
⁷ The righteous are invoked in blessings,
  but the name of the wicked decays.
⁸ The wise in heart accepts commands,
  but the babbling fool comes to ruin.
⁹ Whoever walks in blamelessness walks securely;
  but the one who twists his ways will be known.
¹⁰ He who maliciously winks the eye causes trouble,
  but the babbling fool comes to ruin.
¹¹ The mouth of the righteous is a wellspring of life,
  but the mouth of the wicked conceals violence.
¹² Hatred awakens conflicts,
  but love conceals all transgressions.
¹³ On the lips of an insightful person wisdom is found,
  but a rod is for the back of one who lacks sense.
¹⁴ Wise people store up knowledge,
  but the mouth of a fool is imminent terror.
¹⁵ The wealth of the rich person is his fortified city;
  the terror of poor people is their poverty.
¹⁶ The wage of the righteous is surely life;
  the earnings of the wicked are surely sin and death.

¹⁷ Whoever keeps instruction is a path to life,
  but whoever abandons correction leads astray.
¹⁸ As for the one who conceals hatred with lying lips
  and who publishes an injurious report, he is a fool.
¹⁹ By multiplying words transgression does not cease,
  but whoever restrains his lips is prudent.
²⁰ The tongue of the righteous is choice silver;
  the heart of the wicked is of little worth.
²¹ The lips of a righteous person "shepherd" many,
  but fools die through lack of sense.
²² As for the blessing of the LORD, it brings wealth,
  and he does not add painful toil with it.
²³ To commit villainy is like [the pleasure of] laughter to a fool,
  but wisdom [is like the pleasure of laughter] to an
  understanding person.

²⁴ As for the terror of a wicked person, it will come to him,
   but that which the righteous desire will be given.
²⁵ As soon as the storm passes by, the wicked person is no more,
   but the righteous is an everlasting foundation.
²⁶ As vinegar to the teeth and as smoke to the eyes,
   so is the sluggard to those who send him.
²⁷ The fear of the Lord adds days,
   but the years of the wicked are short.
²⁸ The expectation of the righteous ends in joy,
   but the hope of the wicked perishes.
²⁹ The way of the Lord is a mountain fortress for the blameless,
   but terror for those who do iniquity.
³⁰ The righteous person is never toppled,
   and the wicked will not dwell in the earth.
³¹ The mouth of the righteous yields wisdom,
   but the tongue of perverse people will be cut out.
³² The lips of the righteous person know what is pleasing,
   but the mouth of the wicked [know] what is perverse.

 ## Reflections

IDENTIFYING A VERSE

Write out the verse that stood out to you from this chapter.

_____

_____

_____

Why did it stand out to you?

_____

_____

_____

_____

GOING DEEPER

Read 10:1–5; 15–16; 22. In your own words, what do these five verses teach about diligent work? (What does it produce? What is its opposite? How is it identified? etc.)

_____

_____

_____

Is the result of hard work merely the fruit of personal effort and discipline? In 10:1–5, 22, what role does the Lord play in regard to diligence and blessing?

_____

_____

_____

In your lifetime, how have you seen the Lord provide for your needs—perhaps through your efforts or even in spite of them?

_____

_____

_____

_____

What did you learn about the Lord through the way he provided for you?

_____

_____

_____

_____

APPLYING THE GOSPEL

Read Proverbs 10:12, 1 Corinthians 13:7, and Romans 4:7 (below). How do these passages connect to each other?

_____

_____

_____

As the living embodiment of ultimate wisdom and love, how does Jesus handle the failures and sins of his people?

_____

_____

_____

PERSONALIZING A PRAYER

Take a moment to consider both your and _____'s limitations in living wisely and righteously, and also Christ's generous forgiveness. How do these realities move your heart to give thanks to God and make requests of him? Write out a prayer for yourself and _____ using Proverbs 10 and Romans 4:7.

> "Blessed are those whose lawless deeds are forgiven,
>   and whose sins are covered." (Romans 4:7)

_____

_____

_____

SHARING YOUR STORY

The theme of work fills this chapter of Proverbs. What was your first job outside the home? How did you get this job? What were your responsibilities? Did anything surprise you about it? What lessons did you learn from it? (Include any stories that come to mind.)

_____

_____

_____

_____

_____

_____

_____

Over the years, what jobs have you had which you found most satisfying? Why?

_____

_____

_____

_____

What jobs have been least rewarding? Why?

_____

_____

_____

_____

What skills or aptitudes do you see in the final owner of this journal, which may serve him or her well in work and service?

_____

_____

_____

_____

✒ Proverbs Eleven

Guided Tour

Chapter 11 extends what the previous chapter started. Using the word "but" as a hinge between the first and second lines of most verses, this chapter continues to show how the way of the wise differs from the way of the foolish. This chapter also continues to discuss the contrasting outcomes which lie at the end of these two pathways—the blessing of security resulting from wisdom and the tragedy of consequences resulting from folly. There's an even more drastic distinction between a wise person and a foolish person than you might expect. A wise person is not just insightful, he is also repeatedly (15 times!) called "righteous," while the foolish person is also called "wicked." This means that unwise or "bad choices" are actually sins against God (going our own way and not conforming to his Word). The way of folly is actually the road of rebellion against God. Therefore, foolishness is serious error, and wisdom must be pursued by all those who "fear the LORD." In preparation for the Reflection section, as you read Proverbs 11, mark all the places where a righteous life is identified, encouraged, or contrasted. Regarding its structure, this chapter loosely divides into three sections, each highlighting different expressions of "righteousness" or integrity: righteous blessings (11:1–8); righteous words (11:9–14); and righteous financial dealings (11:15–31). Specific topics to notice in this chapter include: (1) the effect of our words upon others (11:9–14) and (2) the blessing of doing good to others (11:15–18, 23–26).

AT-A-GLANCE

11:1–8	Blessings of Integrity in Actions
11:9–14	Blessings of Integrity in Words
11:15–31	Generosity and Integrity in Finances

¹ Deceptive balances are an abomination to the LORD,
  but a full weight finds his favor.

² Pride comes, and then comes disgrace,
  but with modest people is wisdom.
³ The integrity of the upright leads them,
  but the perversity of the treacherous devastates them.
⁴ Wealth does not profit in the day of wrath,
  but righteousness delivers from death.
⁵ The righteousness of the blameless makes his way straight,
  but by his own wickedness the wicked falls.
⁶ The righteousness of the upright delivers them,
  but through [their] craving the treacherous are captured.
⁷ When a human being dies, hope perishes,
  and the expectation from strength perishes.
⁸ A righteous person is delivered from adversity,
  and the wicked person comes in his place.

⁹ With the mouth the deceiver destroys his neighbor,
  but through knowledge the righteous deliver themselves.
¹⁰ In the prosperity of the righteous a city exults,
   and when the wicked perish, there is a shout of praise.
¹¹ By the blessing of the upright a city is exalted,
   but by the mouth of the wicked it is destroyed.
¹² A person who has no sense despises his neighbor,
   but an understanding person holds his tongue.
¹³ He who goes about as a slanderer is one who reveals a secret,
   but he who is faithful in spirit is one who conceals a word.
¹⁴ Where there is no guidance a people falls,
   but safety [lies] in a multitude of counselors.

¹⁵ One suffers harm grievously when one becomes surety for a stranger,
   but one who hates clapping [hands] is one who is secure.
¹⁶ A gracious woman lays hold of honor,
   but violent men lay hold of wealth.
¹⁷ A kind person is one who rewards himself,
   but the cruel person is one who harms his own flesh.
¹⁸ A wicked person is one who works for a deceptive wage,
   but one who sows righteousness [works for] true pay.
¹⁹ Yes, indeed! The righteous attains life,
   but the one who pursues evil attains his death.
²⁰ People with perverse hearts are an abomination to the Lord,
   but those who are blameless in their way find his favor.

²¹ Be sure of this: an evil person will not go unpunished,
   but such as are righteous will escape.
²² [Like] a gold ring in the snout of a pig [is]
   a beautiful woman who turns aside from discretion.
²³ The desire of the righteous is only good,
   but the hope of the wicked is wrath
²⁴ There is one who scatters and who is increased still more,
   and one who withholds from what is right and comes only to lack.
²⁵ A life bestowing blessing will be fattened,
   and as for the one who drenches, he in turn will be soaked.
²⁶ As for the one who withholds grain, people curse him,
   but blessing [is] on the head of the one who sells it.
²⁷ The one who diligently seeks good will find favor,
   but as for him who searches for evil, it will come to him.
²⁸ As for the one who relies on his wealth, he will fall.
   but like foliage the righteous sprout.
²⁹ The one who ruins his household inherits wind,
   and a fool is a slave to the wise in heart.
³⁰ The fruit of a righteous person is a tree of life,
   and the one who "takes lives" is wise.
³¹ If the righteous person is repaid in the earth,
   how much more the wicked and the sinner.

 Reflections

IDENTIFYING A VERSE

Write out the verse that stood out to you from this chapter.

_____

_____

_____

Why did it stand out to you?

_____

_____

_____

_____

GOING DEEPER

As you read this chapter, mark all the places where righteous living is identified, encouraged, and contrasted? Use these verses to make a list describing the way of righteousness.

_____

_____

_____

_____

In your own words, what are at least three outcomes of righteous living which show its value? (There are more than three in this chapter, so you can add more if you wish.)

_____

_____

_____

_____

Can you think of a time when the Lord helped you do the right thing ("righteous living") even when it was difficult? What happened? And can you see now how the Lord worked it out for good?

_____

_____

_____

_____

CONNECTING THE GOSPEL

Read Proverbs 11:4 and 1 Thessalonians 1:9–10; 5:9. According to these verses, how should the Christian think about the coming day of God's wrath?

_____

_____

_____

Whose righteousness will deliver you from death (Romans 3:21–25, below)?

_____

_____

_____

Explain to _____ how you first came to believe that you needed the righteousness of Christ, instead of your own good works to save you?

_____

_____

_____

_____

PERSONALIZING A PRAYER

Write out a prayer for yourself and _____ using some portion of Proverbs 11 and Romans 3:21–22. Ask God to fill you and _____ with a deep awareness that God sees you as righteous because of Jesus. Thank him that because Jesus bore the wrath of God for us, we don't need to fear the day of God's wrath.

> But now the righteousness of God has been manifested apart from the law, although the Law and the Prophets bear witness to it— the

righteousness of God through faith in Jesus Christ for all who believe. (Romans 3:21–22)

_____

_____

_____

_____

SHARING YOUR STORY

As you consider your "desires" (11:23), what would you say is/has been the mission or purpose of your life? How did you come to have this purpose? And how has it changed from when you were in your twenties and through your thirties and forties and later?

_____

_____

_____

_____

Why would you recommend (or not recommend) this purpose in life to _____?

_____

_____

_____

_____

🖋 Proverbs Twelve

Guided Tour

The chapter begins and ends with generalized reminders about the outcomes which result from pursuing wisdom or folly. Between these bookends, much of the chapter focuses on how someone can get ahead in life. Men and women succeed by wise use of two main resources: their work and their words. The first twelve verses mainly emphasize godly work in different settings: in the family (12:4, 7, 9), in advance planning (12:2–3, 5, 8), in creation care (12:10), and farm life (12:11–12). Verses 13–23 mainly consider the wise use of words. With their words, men and women succeed by honest truth (12:17, 19–20, 22), wise advice (12:15, 18, 23), and kind speech (12:18, 20). Verses 24–27 recap the two topics featured in 12:2–12 and 12:13–23 by combining the themes of "work" and "words" within this four-verse wrap-up.

AT-A-GLANCE

12:1	Introduction
12:2–12	Emphasizing Godly Work
12:13–23	Emphasizing Wise Words
12:24–27	Reemphasizing Work and Words
12:28	Conclusion

¹ One who loves instruction is one who loves knowledge,
   but one who hates correction is an ignoramus.

² A good person obtains favor from the LORD,
   but the crafty he condemns.
³ A human being is not established through wickedness,
   but righteous people are not uprooted.
⁴ A noble and virtuous wife is the crown of her husband,
   but like rottenness in his bones is a shameful wife.
⁵ The plans of righteous people are [toward] justice,

the guidance of wicked people is [toward] deceit.
⁶ The words of wicked people are a bloody ambush,
but the mouth of upright people delivers them.
⁷ Overturn wicked people, and they are no more;
but the household of righteous people stands firm.
⁸ According to his prudence a person is praised,
but the one with a warped mind will be held in contempt.
⁹ Better to be one who is held as worthless and yet has a slave,
than to be one who exalts himself and is one who lacks bread.
¹⁰ A righteous person is one who knows the desires of his animal,
but the mercy of the wicked is cruel.
¹¹ One who works his land is filled with food,
but one who pursues fantasies has no sense.
¹² The wicked person desires the stronghold of evil people,
but the root of righteous people endures.

¹³ In the transgression of [his] lips is the trap set for an evil man,
and so the righteous escapes from distress.
¹⁴ From the fruit of his mouth a person is filled with good things,
and the deeds of one's hands return to him.
¹⁵ The way of a fool is right in his eyes,
but a wise person is one who listens to counsel.
¹⁶ As for a fool, his vexation is revealed on the same day,
but the shrewd person ignores an insult.
¹⁷ A trustworthy witness declares what is right,
but a perjurer [declares] deceit.
¹⁸ There is one who speaks recklessly like the stabbing of a sword,
but the tongue of wise people is a remedy.
¹⁹ A truthful lip is established forever,
but a lying tongue is [only] for a moment.
²⁰ Deceit is in the heart of those who plan evil,
but those who counsel peace have joy.
²¹ No sort of malevolence will happen to the righteous person,
but wicked people are full of harm.
²² Lying lips are an abomination to the LORD,
but those who show trustworthiness find his favor.
²³ A shrewd person is one who conceals knowledge,
but the heart of fools cries out folly.

²⁴ The hand of diligent people will rule,
  but the slack person will become compulsory labor.
²⁵ Anxiety in an individual's heart weighs it down,
  but a good word cheers it up.
²⁶ A righteous man searches out his confidential friend,
  but the way of wicked men leads them astray.
²⁷ A slack person does not roast any game for himself,
  but a diligent person [roasts] the precious wealth of the land.

²⁸ In the path of righteousness is life,
  and the journey of its byway is immortality.

 Reflections

IDENTIFYING A VERSE

Write out the verse that stood out to you from this chapter.

_____

_____

_____

Why did it stand out to you?

_____

_____

_____

_____

GOING DEEPER

Read 12:13–23; 25–26, and list all the activities of the mouth, mentioned in these verses (e.g., speaking truth, 12:17; not speaking, 12:23; leading astray, 12:26; etc.)

_____

_____

_____

Describe one specific struggle you have had with how you use your words.

_____

_____

_____

_____

Describe how the Lord has taught and helped you in this struggle.

_____

_____

_____

_____

CONNECTING THE GOSPEL

Read Proverbs 12:2. Whose life is truly good and pleasing to God the Father? (See Matthew 3:17; 17:5.)

_____

_____

_____

According to Colossians 1:13–14 (below), how are you enabled to benefit from this favored life?

_____

_____

_____

PERSONALIZING A PRAYER

Write out a prayer for yourself and _____ using part of Proverbs 12 and Colossians 1:13–14. Thank God for what he has delivered you from, and ask him to give you and _____ a new (or renewed) life full of wise words and faithfulness that resembles Jesus.

> He has delivered us from the domain of darkness and transferred us to the kingdom of his beloved Son, in whom we have redemption, the forgiveness of sins. (Colossians 1:13–14)

_____

_____

_____

_____

SHARING YOUR STORY

We all need other people (12:25–26). Who was your best friend in elementary school? High school? College?

_____

_____

_____

_____

Do you still keep in touch with them? Why or why not?

_____

_____

_____

_____

What do you remember about them? How would they describe you back then?

_____

_____

_____

_____

What have you learned about being a good friend? Is there anything you would like to have done differently in those friendships?

_____

_____

_____

_____

✒ Proverbs Thirteen

Guided Tour

In keeping with its surrounding chapters (10–15), Proverbs 13 continues to use two-line sayings in which the first and second lines contrast ("opposing parallelism"). The chapter falls into four sections, each organized loosely around a topic: words (13:1–6); wealth (13:7–11); satisfaction (13:12–19); and destiny (13:20–25). Yet spanning these sections, three primary themes recur: (1) receiving the instruction of others (13:1, 10, 13, 14, 18, 20, 24); (2) enjoying the blessings of creation (13:2, 4, 7, 8, 11, 12, 19, 21–23, 25); (3) and noting the God-ordained consequences of choices (13:3, 5, 6, 9, 11, 12, 15–18, 20, 23, 25). In other words, this chapter deals with (1) your relationship with parents (or teachers), (2) your relationship with God's world, and (3) your relationship, ultimately, with God himself. Though God is not specifically mentioned in this chapter, Solomon uses these three recurring themes to teach the careful reader about the virtues which God desires in us and the vices he detests.

AT-A-GLANCE

13:1–6	Words
13:7–11	Wealth
13:12–19	Satisfaction
13:20–25	Destiny

¹ A wise son [listens to] a father's instruction,
  but a mocker does not listen to rebuke.
² From the fruit of a person's mouth one eats good things,
  but the appetite of the treacherous is violence.
³ He who guards his mouth is one who protects his life,
  but as for the one who opens his lips wide, he has terror.
⁴ The sluggard's appetite craves, and he has not;
  but the life of the diligent is fattened.
⁵ A righteous person hates a false word,

but a wicked person becomes a stench and comes to feel ashamed.
⁶ Righteousness guards the blameless way,
  but wickedness overturns the sinful [way].

⁷ There is one who pretends to be rich, yet has nothing;
  and [there is] one who pretends to be poor, yet has great wealth.
⁸ The ransom of a person's life is his riches,
  but a poor person does not listen to a rebuke.
⁹ The light of righteous people shines brightly,
  but the lamp of wicked people is snuffed out.
¹⁰ There is strife only with pride,
  but with those who take counsel [there is] wisdom.
¹¹ Wealth [gotten] by unsound means dwindles,
  but he who gathers by hand increases [his wealth].

¹² Expectation deferred causes the heart to become sick,
  but a tree of life is desire fulfilled.
¹³ The one who despises an [inspired] word will be ruined by it,
  but as for the one who fears a commandment, he will be requited.
¹⁴ The teaching of the wise is a wellspring of life,
  turning [one] aside from the snares of death.
¹⁵ Good judgment wins favor,
  but the way of the treacherous leads to their destruction.
¹⁶ Every shrewd person takes cover through knowledge,
  but a fool spreads out folly.
¹⁷ A wicked messenger perishes through evil,
  but a faithful envoy is one who brings healing.
¹⁸ The person who ignores instruction meets with poverty and disgrace,
  but the one who heeds correction will be honored.
¹⁹ A desire that comes to pass is pleasant to the soul,
  but an abomination to fools is to depart from evil.

²⁰ Walk with the wise and become wise,
  for whoever associates with fools suffers harm.
²¹ Trouble pursues sinners,
  but good things reward the righteous.
²² A good person gives [wealth] as an inheritance to his grandchildren,
  but the wealth of a sinner is stored up for the righteous person.
²³ The unplowed field of poor people yields plenty of food,
  but there is a being swept away through injustice.

²⁴ The one who holds back his rod is one who hates his son,
   but the one who loves him seeks him diligently with discipline.
²⁵ A righteous person is one who eats to the satisfying of his appetite,
   but the belly of the wicked lacks [bread].

 Reflections

IDENTIFYING A VERSE

Write out the verse that stood out to you from this chapter.

_____

_____

_____

Why did it stand out to you?

_____

_____

_____

_____

GOING DEEPER

What does a wise person do, according to the second half of 13:10?

_____

_____

_____

The person who doesn't live out the wisdom showcased in second half of 13:10, will instead encounter strife (interpersonal conflict). According to the first half of 13:10, what's the cause of this relational friction?

_____

_____

_____

In your own experience, when have you found it difficult to receive the advice of others? Why?

_____

_____

_____

_____

How has the Lord taught (or is still teaching) you to humbly accept the advice of other people?

_____

_____

_____

_____

When you find yourself receiving advice from others, *how* do you handle their input? What truths do you try to call to mind, or actions you may take, or words you hope you'll say?

_____

_____

_____

_____

CONNECTING THE GOSPEL

Read Proverbs 13:1—Compare this verse to the description of Jesus found in John 5:36. Though Jesus perfectly modeled the highest of wisdom and obedience to his Father, why did he experience the outcome

typically reserved for the worst of fools (cf. Proverbs 13:18–21)? See
Romans 4:5 and 1 Peter 2:24 (below).

_____

_____

_____

_____

PERSONALIZING A PRAYER

Write out a prayer for yourself and _____ using Proverbs 13:18–21;
Romans 4:5; and 1 Peter 2:24. Thank God for how he has healed your
wounds. Ask him to give you and _____ wisdom in the specific
areas mentioned in Proverbs 13.

> And to the one who does not work but believes in him who justifies
> the ungodly, his faith is counted as righteousness. (Romans 4:5)

> He himself bore our sins in his body on the tree, that we might
> die to sin and live to righteousness. By his wounds you have been
> healed. (1 Peter 2:24)

_____

_____

_____

_____

SHARING YOUR STORY

Wisdom often brings the opportunity to delight in "good things" (13:2).
What do you enjoy doing in your leisure time (hobbies, recreation, pursuits, etc.)? Why?

_____

_____

_____

_____

What in your life do you wish you had spent less time doing (or more time doing)?

_____

_____

_____

_____

What's one fun thing you remember doing with _____? Describe what you did together and why you enjoyed it.

_____

_____

_____

_____

✒ Proverbs Fourteen

Guided Tour

Chapter 14 makes a good point about life: things are not always as they seem (14:12). Sometimes the foolish deviously mask their ways (14:5, 8), or they appear to be busy and engaged in wise pursuits when they are actually doing the opposite (14:1, 6). Other times, the course of folly appears to be wise and blessed, while the path of wisdom seems surrounded by trouble and grief (14:4, 11–14). This is a regular emphasis within the first fourteen verses of this chapter. Note all the places where this theme of "mistaken appearances" occurs. The final twenty-one verses repeatedly use sharp contrasts ("but") to help correct the illusion of the "mistaken appearances" found in 14:1–14. The first fourteen verses tell us what things may look like, but the last twenty-one verses reveal the way things truly are. In this God-created reality, all decisions have unavoidable consequences. Notice throughout this section how often wisdom and righteousness are said to lead to life, while folly and wickedness lead to ruin.

AT-A-GLANCE

14:1–14	Focus on Mistaken Appearances
14:15–35	Focus on Actual Realities

¹ As for the wise among women, [each] builds her house,
  but a foolish woman with her own hands tears it down.
² Whoever fears the LORD walks in his being upright,
  but whoever despises him is perverse in his ways.
³ In the mouth of a fool is a rod of pride,
  but the lips of the wise protect them.
⁴ Without cattle the manger is clean,
  but there are abundant harvests through the strength of an ox.
⁵ An honest witness does not lie,
  but a false witness is a perjurer.
⁶ The mocker seeks wisdom, and he has not,
  but knowledge is an easy matter to the discerning.

⁷ Go from the presence of a foolish person,
   for you will not have known lips of knowledge.
⁸ The wisdom of the shrewd is to have insight into his way,
   but the folly of fools is deceit.
⁹ As for fools, each one mocks at guilt,
   but among upright people [there is] favor.
¹⁰ The heart knows its own bitterness,
   and in its joys a stranger does not take part.
¹¹ The house of wicked people will be annihilated,
   but the tent of upright people will bud.
¹² There is a way that is right in a person's judgment,
   but the end of it is the ways to death.
¹³ Even in laughter the heart may ache,
   and the end of rejoicing is grief.
¹⁴ A backslider will be fully punished because of his ways,
   but a good person [will be fully rewarded] for his deeds.

¹⁵ The gullible gives credence to anything,
   but the shrewd person gives heed to his step.
¹⁶ A wise person is one who fears and who turns from evil,
   but a fool is one who gets angry and yet feels secure.
¹⁷ A quick-tempered person commits folly,
   and a schemer is hated.
¹⁸ Gullible people inherit folly,
   but the shrewd are crowned with knowledge.
¹⁹ Evil people will bow down before good people,
   and wicked people at the gates of a righteous person.
²⁰ Even by his neighbor a poor person is hated,
   but the friends of the rich person are many.
²¹ The one who despises his neighbor is a sinner,
   but as for the one who shows favor to the poor, blessed is he.
²² Do not the planners of evil go astray,
   and do not the planners of good meet with reliable kindness?
²³ In all strenuous labor there is profit,
   but empty talk leads only to scarcity.
²⁴ The crown of wise people is their wealth,
   but the folly of fools is folly.
²⁵ A truthful witness is one who delivers lives,
   but the perjurer is deceitful.

²⁶ In the fear of the Lord is a strong security,
   and his children have a refuge.
²⁷ The fear of the Lord is a wellspring of life,
   turning [the wise] from the traps of death.
²⁸ In a multitude of subjects is the splendor of a king,
   but being without a populace fills the potentate with terror.
²⁹ Patience is great competence,
   but a quick temper is that which exalts folly.
³⁰ Life in the entire body is a calm heart,
   but hot passion is rot in the bones.
³¹ The one who oppresses the poor scoffs at his Maker,
   but he who is gracious to the needy honors God.
³² By his own evil the wicked person is thrown down,
   but the righteous takes refuge in the Lord in his dying.
³³ In the heart of the discerning wisdom comes to rest,
   and in the midst of fools she reveals herself.
³⁴ Righteousness exalts a nation,
   but sin is a condemnation to peoples.
³⁵ The king's favor comes to a prudent servant,
   but his fury ruins a shameful [servant].

Reflections

IDENTIFYING A VERSE

Write out the verse that stood out to you from this chapter.

_____

_____

_____

Why did it stand out to you?

_____

_____

_____

GOING DEEPER

List all the examples of "mistaken appearances" that you can find in 14:1–14 (e.g., angry words look like self-protection, 14:3; lower business overhead seems to be wise fiscal policy, 14:4; seeking wisdom appears to be wise, 14:6; laughter sounds like joy, 14:13; etc.).

_____

_____

_____

_____

When have you observed any of these "mistaken appearances" in chapter 14 in your own experience? Or have you seen other specific kinds of things that "appear to be right" (14:12)? Describe one example: What did it look like at first? How did it turn out at the end?

_____

_____

_____

_____

Do any of the verses in 14:15–35 help unmask the "mistaken appearance" you just described? Which one(s)?

_____

_____

_____

_____

What would you want the future owner of this journal to remember about the truth taught in the verse(s) you just listed?

_____

_____

_____

_____

CONNECTING THE GOSPEL

Read Proverbs 14:3. Now read the account of Jesus's trial recorded in Mark 15 (especially vv. 4–5, 15).

If Jesus, who is supremely wise, perfectly lived out Proverbs 14:3 at his trial before Pilate, why did God cause Jesus to experience the precise punishment reserved for fools?

_____

_____

_____

Consider the prophecies about Jesus in Isaiah 50:5–6 and especially 53:4–6 (below). What was the ultimate purpose of Jesus's suffering?

_____

_____

_____

How does Jesus's suffering the fate of the fool impact you (1 Peter 3:18)?

_____

_____

_____

PERSONALIZING A PRAYER

Write out a prayer for yourself and _____ using part of Proverbs 14 and Isaiah 53:4–6. Thank Jesus for carrying your griefs, sorrows, and punishment ("chastisement"). Ask him to forgive you for going your own way, especially in the specific areas mentioned in Proverbs 14.

> Surely he has borne our griefs
>   and carried our sorrows;
> yet we esteemed him stricken,
>   smitten by God, and afflicted.
> But he was pierced for our transgressions;
>   he was crushed for our iniquities;
> upon him was the chastisement that brought us peace,
>   and with his wounds we are healed.
> All we like sheep have gone astray;
>   we have turned—every one—to his own way;
> and the LORD has laid on him
>   the iniquity of us all. (Isaiah 53:4–6)

_____

_____

_____

_____

SHARING YOUR STORY

Proverbs 14:31 acknowledges that this world is filled with good and with evil. What about the world today encourages you?

_____

_____

_____

In contrast, what problems most need to be addressed in the world today?

_____

_____

_____

What would you do to fix them, if you could?

_____

_____

_____

_____

How have you seen _____ working to make this world a better place?

_____

_____

_____

_____

✎ Proverbs Fifteen

Guided Tour

After a brief introduction about the benefits of kind speech (15:1–4), this chapter opens up the windows of a household for us to glimpse inside. The setting of chapter 15 is the family. Notice how often the chapter mentions a parent's instruction or discipline (15:5, 10, 12, 31–33), a house or household, and children. Parental instruction should be valued (15:5–19), because it results in blessing if received, or destruction if refused (15:20–29). And it is through these family relationships that the inner workings of the human heart (15:7, 11, 13–15, 28) are most clearly seen—especially through verbal communication (15:7, 8, 14, 23, 26, 28–30). Parents should try to shape not only a child's external behavior, but also his internal being or "heart." As you read, mark all the mentions of the inward life of a person (e.g., emotions, motives, priorities, etc.). This inner orientation is often revealed through one's speech. Additionally, chapter 15 highlights not only the heart of a child, but also the heart of God. All children (and their parents) must learn and reflect both what God loves and what he hates (15:3, 8, 9, 20–26, 29, 33). How wonderful to learn that one thing he loves is to hear the prayers of his own (15:8, 29).

AT-A-GLANCE

15:1–4	The Benefits of Kind Speech
15:5–19	The Value of Receiving Instruction
15:20–33	The Results of Receiving (or Not Receiving) Instruction

¹ A gentle answer turns back wrath,
   but a painful word stirs up anger.
² The tongue of the wise adorns knowledge,
   but the mouth of fools gushes forth folly.
³ The eyes of the LORD are in every place,
   watching [vigilantly] evil people and good people.

⁴ The soothing of the tongue is a tree of life,
   but perversity in it fractures the spirit.

⁵ A fool spurns his father's instruction,
   but whoever heeds correction is shrewd.
⁶ The house of the righteous is a great store of wealth,
   but in the wages of the wicked is ruin.
⁷ The lips of wise people scatter knowledge;
   the heart of fools is not right.
⁸ The sacrifice of wicked people is an abomination to the LORD,
   but the prayer of upright people finds his favor.
⁹ An abomination to the LORD is the way of the wicked,
   but as for the one who pursues righteousness, he loves.
¹⁰ Painful discipline awaits the one who abandons the path [of life];
   the one who hates correction will die.
¹¹ Sheol and Abaddon are in full view of the LORD;
   how much more the hearts of human beings?
¹² The mocker does not like to be corrected;
   to wise people he does not go.
¹³ A joyful heart makes the face attractive,
   but in heartache is a broken spirit.
¹⁴ A discerning heart seeks knowledge,
   but the mouth of fools feeds on folly.
¹⁵ All the days of the afflicted are wretched,
   but a cheerful heart is a feast continually.
¹⁶ Better a little with the fear of the LORD
   than great treasure and turmoil with it.
¹⁷ Better a small serving of vegetables with love
   than a fattened ox with hatred.
¹⁸ A wrathful person stirs up strife,
   but a patient person pacifies a dispute.
¹⁹ The way of a sluggard is like a briar hedge,
   but the path of upright people is a built-up highway.

²⁰ A wise son makes a glad father,
   but a foolish human being is one who despises his mother.
²¹ Folly brings joy to one who has no sense,
   but an understanding person makes [his] going straight.
²² Plans are thwarted without counsel,
   but with a multitude of counselors each plan succeeds.

^{23} An individual has joy in the apt answer of his mouth,
   and how good is a word at the right time!
^{24} The path of life leads upward for the prudent,
   and so turns aside from the grave below.
^{25} The LORD tears away the house of the proud,
   but he sets in place the boundary of the widow.
^{26} The plans of an evil person are an abomination to the LORD,
   but pleasant words are pure.
^{27} Whoever is greedy for gain is one who ruins his household,
   but the one who hates bribes will live.
^{28} The heart of a righteous person ponders [its] answer,
   but the mouth of wicked people blurts out evil things.
^{29} The LORD is far from the wicked people,
   but he hears the prayer of righteous people.
^{30} The light of the eyes makes the heart glad,
   and good news revives the whole person.
^{31} The ear that listens to life-giving correction
   dwells among the wise.
^{32} The person who flouts instruction is one who despises his life,
   but the person who hears correction is one who acquires sense.
^{33} The instruction that gives wisdom is the fear of the LORD,
   and humility [comes] before honor.

 Reflections

IDENTIFYING A VERSE

Write out the verse that stood out to you from this chapter.

_____

_____

_____

Why did it stand out to you?

_____

_____

GOING DEEPER

List all the things in chapter 15 that displease the Lord.

_____

_____

_____

List all the things in chapter 15 that please the Lord?

_____

_____

_____

In your own words, how would you sum up the heart of the Lord, as revealed in both sets of these verses?

_____

_____

_____

The Lord knows everything about our hearts (what pleases and displeases *us*, 15:3, 11). Since nothing is hidden from him, how would the Lord want you to grow in order to love more of what God loves and hate what he hates? Give specifics (actions, words, prayers, thoughts, etc.).

_____

_____

_____

_____

CONNECTING THE GOSPEL

Read Proverbs 15:8, 29 and compare with John 11:42. How does Jesus fulfill these verses from Proverbs?

_____

_____

_____

_____

Why does God, according to John 16:23–24 (below), listen to the prayers we offer?

_____

_____

_____

_____

PERSONALIZING A PRAYER

Write out a prayer for yourself and _____ using some portion of Proverbs 15 and John 16:23–24. Ask for what you desire, in Jesus's name, for yourself and for _____.

> "In that day you will ask nothing of me. Truly, truly, I say to you, whatever you ask of the Father in my name, he will give it to you. Until now you have asked nothing in my name. Ask, and you will receive, that your joy may be full." (John 16:23–24)

_____

_____

_____

_____

_____

SHARING YOUR STORY

Proverbs 15:13 speaks of both a "joyful heart" and also "heartache." Describe one of the happiest times of your life.

_____

_____

_____

What was the hardest time?

_____

_____

_____

The scariest time?

_____

_____

_____

How did you come to experience these? What made them so significant in your life?

_____

_____

_____

In your experience, what kinds of things in life bring the most lasting happiness?

_____

_____

_____

_____

✒ Proverbs Sixteen

Guided Tour

Chapter 16 divides into two main sections: 16:1–15 and 16:16–30, with the last three verses of the chapter (vv. 31–33) perhaps best fitting with the first six verses of the chapter 17. The first main section of chapter 16 (vv. 1–15) addresses the interrelationship between man's activity and God's authority. Human beings make various kinds of decisions—some good, some bad, some neutral. But every person lives under God's sovereign authority, which at times he exercises directly (providentially guiding and guarding your life, 16:1, 3, 4, 6, 7, 9, 11) and at other times he mediates through a human agency (e.g., governments are supposed to wield and represent God's own authority, 16:10, 12–15). Containing incentives for getting wisdom (like Proverbs 1—9), the second main section of this chapter (16:16–30) mainly features frequent observations about one's speech. On this topic, notice where Solomon places special emphasis: (a) on how one gives or receives words of instruction, (b) on the negative consequences awaiting those who refuse wise instruction, and (c) on the positive benefits of wise speaking.

AT-A-GLANCE

16:1–15	Relationship between Human Activity and God's Authority
16:16–30	Relationship between Receiving Counsel and the Resulting Consequences
16:31–33	(see next chapter)

¹ To human beings belong the plans of the heart;
   from the LORD [comes] the right answer of the tongue.
² All the ways of a person [are] pure in his own eyes,
   but the LORD is the one who evaluates motives.
³ Commit to the LORD your works,
   and your thoughts will be established.

⁴ The Lᴏʀᴅ works everything to its appropriate end,
  even the wicked person for an evil day.
⁵ An abomination to the Lᴏʀᴅ is everyone who is haughty;
  be sure of this, that person will not go unpunished.
⁶ Through love and faithfulness sin is atoned for,
  and through the fear of the Lᴏʀᴅ is a departing from evil.
⁷ When the Lᴏʀᴅ takes pleasure in a person's ways,
  he compels even his enemies to surrender to him.
⁸ Better a little with righteousness
  than a large income with injustice.
⁹ The heart of a human being plans his way,
  but the Lᴏʀᴅ establishes his step.
¹⁰ An inspired verdict is on the king's lips;
  in giving a judgment his mouth is not unfaithful.
¹¹ A just balance and hand scale are the Lᴏʀᴅ's;
  all the weights in a pouch are his work.
¹² An abomination to kings is doing wickedness,
  because a throne is established through righteousness.
¹³ Kings take pleasure in righteous lips,
  and whoever speaks upright things he loves.
¹⁴ The wrath of the king is the messenger of death,
  but a wise person pacifies it.
¹⁵ In the light of the king's face is life,
  and his favor is like a cloud of spring rain.

¹⁶ To acquire wisdom, how much better than gold!
  And to acquire insight is preferable to silver.
¹⁷ The highway of the upright is turning aside from evil;
  the one who protects his life is one who guards his way.
¹⁸ Before a shattering comes pride,
  and before humiliation, a haughty spirit.
¹⁹ Better to be lowly in spirit with the oppressed
  than to divide plunder with the proud.
²⁰ The one who pays attention to a saying finds good,
  and as for the one who trusts in the Lᴏʀᴅ, blessed is he!
²¹ The wise of heart is named "Insightful,"
  and sweetness of lips increases persuasiveness.
²² A wellspring of life is prudence to those who have it,
  but the discipline of fools is folly.
²³ The heart of the wise causes his mouth to be prudent,

and on his lips he adds persuasiveness.
²⁴ Pleasant words are overflowing honey,
  sweet to the soul and a remedy to the bones.
²⁵ There is a way that is right in a person's judgment,
  but the end of it is ways to death.
²⁶ The appetite of the toiler toils for him;
  surely his mouth urges him on.
²⁷ A troublemaker is one who prepares mischief,
  and on his lip [it] is like a scorching fire.
²⁸ A perverse person unleashes conflict,
  and the slanderer is one who alienates a close friend.
²⁹ A violent person entices his companion
  and leads him in a way that is not good.
³⁰ Blinking his eyes, he devises perversity;
  pursing his lips, he brings evil to pass.

 Reflections

IDENTIFYING A VERSE

Write out the verse that stood out to you from this chapter.

_____

_____

_____

Why did it stand out to you?

_____

_____

_____

GOING DEEPER

What qualities do 16:8, 16, 19 say are "better"? List all three in the left side of the table below.

These qualities are superior to something. What are they better than? List these inferior aspects in the right side of the table below.

	Better	Inferior
16:8		
16:16		
16:19		

In your own words, what is the allure of each inferior aspect you just listed? What makes each seem to be better (though it's not)?

16:8 _____

_____

_____

16:16 _____

_____

_____

16:19 _____

_____

_____

How have you personally observed these "better" qualities actually turn out to be superior? Share with _____ how and when you've seen God demonstrate his way to be superior to the inferior ways you just listed.

_____

_____

_____

_____

_____

CONNECTING THE GOSPEL

Read Proverbs 16:6. According to John 1:14 (below), how did Jesus perfectly qualify to atone for sin?

_____

_____

_____

How did Jesus's love and faithfulness atone for your sin?

_____

_____

_____

How has that changed your outlook and life?

_____

_____

_____

PERSONALIZING A PRAYER

Write out a prayer for yourself and _____ using part of Proverbs 16 and John 1:14. Remember to thank God for his love and faithfulness. Ask for help to recognize his ways in your world and to help _____ also to recognize God's ways in life.

> And the Word became flesh and dwelt among us, and we have seen his glory, glory as of the only Son from the Father, full of grace and truth. (John 1:14)

_____

_____

_____

_____

SHARING YOUR STORY

No human decision occurs outside the realm of God's authority (Proverbs 16:33). As you consider the decisions that have shaped you, what would you identify as major forks in the road of your life?

_____

_____

_____

_____

What were the options and why did you make the decision you did?

_____

_____

_____

_____

How have these turning points affected you and your family?

_____

_____

_____

_____

In your own words, describe an important milestone (a decision or important event) in the life of _____.

_____

_____

_____

_____

✒ Proverbs Seventeen

Guided Tour

The first seven verses of chapter 17 (combined with the last three verses of chapter 16) contain a list of ironies. Each situation presents a striking incongruity or difference between what might be expected and what actually occurs. For example, "gray hair" isn't a sign of weakness, but of splendor (16:31). The roll of the dice seems random, but it's not (16:33). Poverty and peace are better than feasting and friction (17:1). And a wicked person ironically falls prey to wickedness (17:4). Most of the rest of the chapter (17:8–26) could carry the title: "Warning! Warning!" The first half of this "warning" section (17:8–19) broadly addresses relational strife, while the second half (17:20–26) gives repeated attention to the related topics of trouble and sorrow. Additionally, the majority of this entire "warning section" (17:8–26) focuses some attention on the terrible consequences of folly and wickedness, while occasionally presenting the good consequences of wisdom and righteousness (17:9a, 17, 22a, 24a). The final two verses (17:27–28) seem to fit best with the topic addressed in chapter 18.

AT-A-GLANCE

16:31–17:7	Ironies about Life
17:8–19	Warnings about Relationships
17:20–26	Warnings about Calamity
17:27–28	(see next chapter)

16 ³¹ Gray hair is a splendid crown;
   it is found in the way of righteousness.
   ³² Better to be a patient person than a mighty hero,
      even one who rules over his spirit than one who captures a city.
   ³³ Into the bosom the lot is hurled,
      and from the LORD [come] all its decisions.

17 ¹ Better a dry piece of bread with peace and quiet
  than a house full of sacrifices with strife.
  ² A prudent slave rules over a shameful son,
  and receives the inheritance in the midst of the brothers.
  ³ The crucible is for silver, and the furnace for gold,
  but the one who tests hearts is the LORD.
  ⁴ One who pays attention to a malevolent lip is an evildoer;
  one who listens to a destructive tongue is a liar.
  ⁵ The one who mocks the poor person reproaches his Maker;
  the one who rejoices over calamity will not escape punishment.
  ⁶ The [splendid] crown of the aged is children's children,
  and the glorious [crown] of children is their fathers.
  ⁷ An eloquent lip is not fitting for a godless fool;
  how much more unfitting is a lying lip for a nobleman.

  ⁸ A bribe is a magic stone in the eyes of its owner;
  to whomever he turns he thinks he will succeed.
  ⁹ Whoever would foster love is one who covers over a transgression,
  but whoever repeats a matter separates close friends.
  ¹⁰ A rebuke penetrates more deeply into a discerning person
  than flogging a fool a hundred times.
  ¹¹ An evil person fosters only rebellion,
  but a cruel messenger is sent against him.
  ¹² Meet a she-bear robbed of her young by a man,
  but [do] not [meet] a fool in his folly.
  ¹³ As for the one who repays evil for good,
  evil does not depart from his house.
  ¹⁴ The beginning of strife is one who breaks open a dam;
  so before a quarrel breaks out drop the controversy.
  ¹⁵ As for the one who pronounces a wicked person innocent,
  and as for the one who pronounces a righteous person guilty,
  both, yes, both of them are an abomination to the LORD.
  ¹⁶ Why in the world is there payment in the hand of a fool
  to buy wisdom when he has no capacity to learn?
  ¹⁷ At all times a friend is one who loves,
  and a relative is born for adversity.
  ¹⁸ One who claps a palm is a human being who has no sense;
  the one who pledges a security in the presence of his neighbor.

¹⁹ One who loves strife is one who loves transgression,
   and one who makes his doorway high is one who seeks destruction.

²⁰ A person with a perverse heart does not find good,
   and one with a corrupt tongue falls into evil.
²¹ The one who begets a fool brings himself grief,
   and the father of a godless fool does not rejoice.
²² A joyful heart promotes healing,
   but a drained spirit dries up the bone.
²³ A wicked person accepts a bribe from the bosom
   to divert the paths of justice.
²⁴ Wisdom stands ready to serve the discerning,
   but the eyes of a fool are [looking] at the ends of the earth.
²⁵ A foolish son is a vexation to his father
   and brings bitterness to the one who bore him.
²⁶ If even to fine an innocent person is not good,
   how much more flogging nobles is against what is upright.

 Reflections

IDENTIFYING A VERSE

Write out the verse that stood out to you from this chapter.

_____

_____

_____

Why did it stand out to you?

_____

_____

_____

_____

GOING DEEPER

Read 17:8, 9, 13, 19. In your own words, list the various actions that tend to create interpersonal conflict.

_____

_____

_____

According to 17:8, 19, what are two attempts at creating peace, which don't actually work?

_____

_____

_____

_____

According to 17:9, 14, 17, what courses of action tend to genuinely encourage relational peace? (These may occur before or even in the midst of adversity.)

_____

_____

_____

_____

What lessons has the Lord taught you (either from positive or negative experiences) that have helped you avoid or resolve conflict?

_____

_____

_____

_____

CONNECTING THE GOSPEL

Read Proverbs 17:15. In contrast to this verse, explain how God the Father could justly condemn his righteous Son, while also justifying wicked sinners who trust in his Son. Consider the solution offered in 2 Corinthians 5:21 and Galatians 3:13.

_____

_____

_____

_____

PERSONALIZING A PRAYER

Write out a prayer for yourself and _____ using Proverbs 17:8–19. Take a moment to pray for someone you have been in conflict with. Ask God to bless and help him or her. Pray for peace in all of your relationships. Pray for _____ in all of his/her relationships. Using Ephesians 2:13–15, thank God that Jesus is peace and has made peace both between us and God and also between us and others.

> But now in Christ Jesus you who once were far off have been brought near by the blood of Christ. For he himself is our peace, who has made us both one and has broken down in his flesh the dividing wall of hostility by abolishing the law of commandments expressed in ordinances, that he might create in himself one new man in place of the two, so making peace. (Ephesians 2:13–15)

_____

_____

_____

_____

SHARING YOUR STORY

Proverbs 17:6 reminds us of the importance and blessing of family relationships. Write down a few memories of what it was like to grow up in your family:

What were your nicknames? Why?

_____

_____

How did you get along with your siblings?

_____

_____

_____

What was your favorite (or least favorite) family trip? Why?

_____

_____

_____

What churches did you attend, and what were they like or how are they different than the church you attend now?

_____

_____

_____

Did your family have any favorite games (or other pastimes or recipes) you enjoyed together? If so, fill in the details.

_____

_____

_____

How would you want the recipient of this journal and future generations in your family to remember you?

_____

_____

_____

_____

✒ Proverbs Eighteen

Guided Tour

While this chapter doesn't employ many "opposing parallelisms" (which are more prominent in chapters 10–15; see endnote 3), Solomon nonetheless continues to present a contrast, this time between strife and security. Regarding strife, Proverbs 17:27–28; 18:1–8, 17–19 highlight the connection between foolish speech and resultant conflict. For example, a fool creates interpersonal friction through foolish talk, such as: quarreling (17:27–28; 18:1, 6, 18), venting his opinion (18:2, 13), and gossiping (18:8). And this theme finds a summary statement in 18:21: the tongue can be the source of life and blessing on the one hand, or of death and trouble on the other. In contrast to this sort of speech-provoked strife, verses 10–17, 20–21 emphasize the theme of security, which includes safety (18:10), justice (18:17), well-being (18:14, 20–21), and success (18:11–12, 16). The last three verses of chapter 18 begin a theme which continues in chapter 19.

AT-A-GLANCE

17:27–18:8	Foolish Speech and Strife (part one)
18:9–16	Wise Speech and Security
18:17–21	Foolish Speech and Strife (part two)
18:22–24	(see next chapter)

17 ²⁷ One who knows knowledge is one who restrains his words,
　　and an understanding person is cool of spirit.
　²⁸ Even a fool who holds his tongue is thought to be wise;
　　one who stops up his lips, to be discerning.
18 ¹ The one who separates himself seeks self-gratification;
　　against all sound judgment he starts a quarrel.
　² A fool does not delight in understanding
　　but in his heart's exposing itself.
　³ When a wicked person comes, contempt also comes;

and with shame is reproach.
⁴ The words of a person's mouth are deep waters;
  the wellspring of wisdom is a rushing stream.
⁵ To show favoritism to the guilty is not good,
  and so denies the innocent justice.
⁶ The lips of a fool come into controversy,
  and his mouth cries out for beatings.
⁷ The mouth of a fool brings terror to himself,
  and his lips are a trap for his very life.
⁸ The words of a slanderer are like tidbits;
  they descend into one's innermost being.

⁹ Even the one who is slack in his work,
  is a brother of him who destroys.
¹⁰ The name of the Lord is a fortified tower;
  a righteous person runs into it and is protected on high.
¹¹ The wealth of a rich person is his fortified city,
  and like a high city wall in his imagination.
¹² Before destruction a person's heart is high and haughty,
  but before honor is humility.
¹³ As for the one who replies before listening,
  it is to him folly and shame.
¹⁴ A person's spirit can endure even sickness,
  but as for a broken spirit, who can bear it?
¹⁵ The heart of the discerning acquires knowledge,
  for the ears of wise people seek knowledge.
¹⁶ A person's gift makes room for him
  and leads him before great people.

¹⁷ The first to present his case in a dispute seems right,
  until his opponent comes and cross-examines him.
¹⁸ The lot puts an end to conflicts
  and separates powerful [opponents].
¹⁹ An offended brother is like a strong city,
  and conflicts are like the bolt of a citadel.
²⁰ From the fruit of a person's mouth his belly is sated,
  [from] the harvest of his lips he is sated.
²¹ Death and life are in the power of the tongue,
  and those who love it, each will eat its fruit.

 Reflections

IDENTIFYING A VERSE

Write out the verse that stood out to you from this chapter.

_____

_____

_____

Why did it stand out to you?

_____

_____

_____

_____

GOING DEEPER

This chapter includes many descriptions of foolish speech, which result in conflict and trouble. According to 18:11, how do the rich try to avoid trouble? Summarize this verse in your own words.

_____

_____

Why is this approach to dealing with trouble and conflict doomed to fail?

_____

_____

When you encounter conflict and trouble, what is a good response? Read Proverbs 18:10. Summarize this verse, in contrast to your summary of 18:11.

_____

_____

How is the Lord a better refuge in time of trouble, than what is described in 18:11?

_____

_____

In your life where and when have you faced conflict and trouble?

_____

_____

_____

_____

How has the Lord been a refuge for you during these times? As much as possible, give specific examples of what you've faced and how you've found the Lord your refuge.

_____

_____

_____

_____

CONNECTING THE GOSPEL

Read Proverbs 18:4. What has Christ put deep within each believer that is better than mere wisdom, and that will fully and properly relate us to God? (See John 7:37–39.)

_____

_____

How has the Spirit worked in your life to give you refuge from conflict and trouble?

_____

_____

_____

PERSONALIZING A PRAYER

Write out a prayer for yourself and _____ using Proverbs 18:10. Take a moment to pray, giving thanks for the troubles and conflicts he/she has faced and, with the Lord's help, has overcome. Pray for _____ that the Lord will be his/her strong tower in times of future trouble.

> The name of the LORD is a strong tower;
>   the righteous man runs into it and is safe. (Proverbs 18:10)

_____

_____

_____

_____

SHARING YOUR STORY

Throughout the stages of life, troubles come in all shapes and sizes. What did you not like to do when you were growing up?

Least favorite chores around the house

_____

Least favorite subjects in school

_____

Least favorite foods or restaurants

_____

Least favorite family activities

_____

Least favorite pastimes or vacation spots

_____

How did you handle the things you didn't like to do?

_____

_____

_____

_____

What would you want _____ to remember when going through difficulties in his or her life?

_____

_____

_____

_____

🪶 Proverbs Nineteen

Guided Tour

A huge cast of characters walks through the twenty-nine verses of chapter 19 (along with the last three verses of chapter 18). You will meet a wife (18:22; 19:14), children (19:13, 18, 26–27), the poor (18:23; 19:1, 17), friends (18:24; 19:4, 6), a false witness (19:5, 9, 28), a king (19:6, 12), the sluggard (19:24), the mocker (19:25, 29), and more. All of your real-life interactions with these individuals should be done in faithfulness (18:24; 19:1, 5, 9, 15, 16, 18, 24, 25, 28, 29) and in mercy (18:23; 19:4, 7, 11, 17, 22, 26). All of these your interpersonal interactions stand in contrast to your personal life of the heart, which also receives attention in this chapter. These inner dynamics include your desires (19:2), your core self (19:3, 21), your love (19:8), your glory (19:11), your hatred (19:16), your contentment (19:23), and your shame (19:26). Through examples from the interior (personal) and exterior (interpersonal) life, notice how Solomon gives contour and definition to the problems facing the poor (18:23–19:10); the facets of a godly life (19:11–24); and the nature of the Mocker (19:25–29; see "A Bird's-Eye View of Proverbs," page 12, for more on the Mocker).

AT-A-GLANCE

18:22–19:10	The Problems Facing the Poor
19:11–24	The Facets of a Godly Life
19:25–29	The Nature of the Mocker

18 ²² One who finds a wife finds good,
    and so obtains favor from the Lord.
  ²³ The poor speaks pleadingly,
    but the rich answers rudely.
  ²⁴ A person who has unreliable companions is about to be broken,
    but there is a friend who sticks closer than a brother.

19 ¹ Better is a poor person who walks in his integrity
  than one who twists his lips, for he is a fool.
² If even desire without knowledge is not good,
  how much more will the one who hastens with his feet miss the way.
³ The folly of a human being overturns his way,
  but his heart rages against the LORD.
⁴ Wealth attracts many companions,
  but as for the poor person, his close companion separates himself.
⁵ A perjurer will not escape punishment,
  and a witness to lies will not escape.
⁶ Many seek the favor of a nobleman,
  and the generous person has everyone for a companion.
⁷ Every one of the poor person's brothers hates him,
  how much more his close companion becomes distant from him.
  Though he pursues them with pleadings, they are not to be found.
⁸ The one who gets sense is one who loves his life;
  the one who heeds understanding will soon find what is good.
⁹ A perjurer will not escape punishment,
  and a witness to lies will perish.
¹⁰ Luxury is not fitting for a fool;
  how much more [unfitting] for a slave to rule over princes.

¹¹ A human being's prudence yields patience,
  and his splendor is to pass over transgression.
¹² The roaring as of a lion is the fury of a king,
  but like dew on vegetation is his favor.
¹³ A foolish son is destruction for his father,
  and a wife's quarrelings are a leaky roof that drips constantly.
¹⁴ A household and wealth are an inheritance from fathers;
  but from the LORD is a prudent wife.
¹⁵ Laziness casts [one] into a deep sleep,
  and a slack person hungers.
¹⁶ The one who keeps a commandment is one who preserves his life,
  but the one who despises his ways will die.
¹⁷ The one who shows grace to the poor is one who lends to the LORD;
  and as for his deeds, he will repay him.
¹⁸ Discipline your son, for surely there is hope,
  and to killing him do not set your desire.
¹⁹ A hothead is one who incurs a penalty;
  surely if you deliver [him], you will do so again.

²⁰ Listen to counsel and receive discipline
  so that you may be counted among the wise in your final destiny.
²¹ The plans in the heart of a person are many,
  but as for the counsel of the Lord, it will take place.
²² What people desire in a human being is his unfailing kindness;
  better is a poor person than a liar.
²³ The fear of the Lord is surely life;
  fully satisfied, he dwells not met with harm.
²⁴ The sluggard buries his hand in the pan;
  to his mouth he does not return it.

²⁵ Flog a mocker, and the gullible will become prudent;
  and if one corrects the insightful, he discerns knowledge.
²⁶ The one who ruins [his] father, driving out [his] mother,
  is a shameful and disgraceful son.
²⁷ Cease, my son, listening to instruction
  in order to stray from the words of knowledge!
²⁸ A corrupt witness mocks at justice,
  and the mouth of the wicked swallows iniquity.
²⁹ Punishments are established for mockers,
  and beatings for the back of fools.

 ## Reflections

IDENTIFYING A VERSE

Write out the verse that stood out to you from this chapter.

_____

_____

_____

Why did it stand out to you?

_____

_____

_____

GOING DEEPER

Read 19:8, 16, 20, 25, 27, 29. According to these verses, describe to _____ what his/her lifelong response should be to wise instruction.

_____

_____

_____

According to the same verses, summarize how fools respond to counsel and advice.

_____

_____

_____

These same verses also describe the consequences for those who refuse to heed wise counsel. How would you describe these consequences? How have you seen this played out—either in your own life or the life of someone else?

_____

_____

_____

Describe the kind of person who graciously receives words of instruction or advice (their attitude, responses, words, actions, demeanor, heart-posture, etc.).

_____

_____

_____

How has receiving another person's advice positively affected you or some other person you know? Describe.

_____

_____

_____

CONNECTING THE GOSPEL

Read Proverbs 19:17. According to Proverbs 19:17, why is it good to be generous? What are some reasons that it is hard for people to be generous?

_____

_____

_____

_____

Read Matthew 25:31–46 (especially v. 40, below) and Luke 7:36–50 (especially v. 47). What does how you spend your money reveal about you and what you care most about?

_____

_____

_____

_____

PERSONALIZING A PRAYER

Write out a prayer for yourself and _____ using some portion of Proverbs 19 and Matthew 25:40. Ask God to give you and _____ generous hearts. Ask for forgiveness for the times you haven't been generous. Thank the King for his generosity to us (Luke 7:47–50).

> "And the King will answer them, 'Truly, I say to you, as you did it to one of the least of these my brothers, you did it to me.'" (Matthew 25:40)

_____

_____

_____

_____

SHARING YOUR STORY

Limitations aren't always bad (for example, notice how Proverbs 19:1, 22 positively portray the limitation of poverty). God has given each of us limitations (physical, intellectual, financial, etc.). Some difficulties might be avoided by living within our limitations. How has knowing your limitations helped you in life?

_____

_____

_____

_____

Describe for the future owner of this journal how you came to realize some of your limitations.

_____

_____

_____

_____

✒ Proverbs Twenty

Guided Tour

Chapter 20 divides into two main sections: 20:1–19 and 20:20–30. Throughout the first main section, Solomon once again analyzes both how things appear to be and also how things really are (see chapter 14). Regarding appearances, for example, while it seems to make sense to fight over offended honor, it's actually more honorable to avoid strife (20:3). Similarly, other people may possess a depth that isn't obvious at first glance (20:5). And not everyone who claims to love you actually does (20:6). Alternating with these observations about "appearances" are straightforward declarations about what is really true. For example, when a king gets angry, it's not merely for show—so take cover (20:2). Further truths assert that loving sleep leads to poverty (20:13), befriending a talkative gossip brings trouble (20:19), and living in genuine integrity may not be fully enjoyed for a generation (20:7). Regardless of appearances, the real truth about a person will be discerned (20:8–12). The second main section (20:20–30) switches attention to a person's authorities. How should you respond to those who have authority over you? This list of authorities includes: the Lord (20:22–25, 27), rulers (20:26, 28, 30), and older generations, including parents (20:20–21, 29).

AT-A-GLANCE

20:1–19	Appearances and Realities
20:20–30	Authorities and Responses

¹ Wine is a mocker and beer is a brawler;
  and everyone who staggers by them is not wise.
² The roaring as of a lion is the terror struck by the king;
  whoever angers him forfeits his life.
³ Abstaining from strife brings glory to the individual,
  but every fool starts a quarrel.
⁴ A sluggard does not plow from winter on;

then he asks for [a crop] in the harvest, but there is none.
⁵ The counsel in a person's heart is deep waters,
  but an understanding person draws it out.
⁶ As for many human beings, each person proclaims his unfailing kindness.
  But a conscientious person who can find?
⁷ As for one who walks in his blamelessness as a righteous person,
  blessed are his children after him.
⁸ A king is one who sits on a throne of judgment,
  winnowing all evil with his eyes.
⁹ Who can say, "I have cleansed my heart;
  I am pure from my sin"?
¹⁰ As for diverse weights [and] diverse ephahs —
  indeed, both of them are an abomination to the LORD.
¹¹ Even a youth in his evil deeds dissembles.
  So is his conduct pure, or is it upright?
¹² As for the hearing ear and the seeing eye,
  indeed, both of them the LORD has made.
¹³ Do not love sleep lest you become poor.
  Open your eyes and be filled with food.
¹⁴ "Bad, bad," says the buyer—
  and when he has it in hand, then he boasts.
¹⁵ There is gold and an abundance of corals,
  but a precious vessel is lips that speak knowledge.
¹⁶ Take away his garment when one becomes surety for a stranger;
  and for an outsider impound it.
¹⁷ Food gotten by deceit is sweet to the person,
  but afterward his mouth is filled with gravel.
¹⁸ Plans are established with counsel,
  so with guidance make war.
¹⁹ He who goes about as a slanderer divulges secrets,
  so do not get involved with a silly chatterer.

²⁰ As for the one who curses his father and his mother,
  his lamp will be snuffed out in pitch darkness.
²¹ As for an inheritance gained in haste at the beginning,
  in its latter end it will not be blessed.
²² Do not say, "I will repay evil!"
  Look expectantly to the LORD, and he will avenge you.

^{23} An abomination to the LORD, are diverse weights,
   and deceptive balances are not good.
^{24} From the LORD are the steps of a man;
   and as for a human being, how can he understand his way?
^{25} A trap for a human being is one who says rashly, "Consecrated,"
   and after [making] the vows to examine [them].
^{26} The wise king winnows the wicked,
   and brings back the cartwheel over them.
^{27} The words of a human being are the lamp of the LORD,
   shedding light on his innermost parts.
^{28} Kindness and reliability guard the king;
   he upholds his throne with kindness.
^{29} The splendor of choice young men is their strength,
   and the majesty of the aged is their gray hair.
^{30} Bruising wounds scour away evil,
   and blows [polish] the innermost being.

 Reflections

IDENTIFYING A VERSE

Write out the verse that stood out to you from this chapter.

_____

_____

_____

Why did it stand out to you?

_____

_____

_____

GOING DEEPER

What is the Lord like, according to 20:10, 12, 22, 23? List at least three things.

_____

_____

_____

Although the Lord alone is responsible for taking revenge against injustice, how would you describe the response to injustice which God desires from his children (20:22)?

_____

_____

_____

How would you describe what else the Lord expects from his children according to 20:10, 23?

_____

_____

_____

Where and when in your life have you experienced injustice, even when you were trying to do the right thing? Describe what happened and how you felt.

_____

_____

_____

Have your own weaknesses, mistakes and/or sins complicated how you've tried to deal with the situation you just described? In spite of these, how has the Lord helped you through that situation? (How has he worked to set things right or given you grace to be forgiving and patient?)

_____

_____

_____

_____

CONNECTING THE GOSPEL

Read Proverbs 20:9. What answers has God given to the questions asked in this verse? Take time to consider Leviticus 16:30; Psalm 51:2, 10–12 (below); and 1 John 1:7, as you write out your answer.

_____

_____

_____

_____

PERSONALIZING A PRAYER

Write out a prayer for yourself and _____ using parts of Proverbs 20 and Psalm 51:10–12. Thank the Lord for the sacrifice of his Son, which makes us clean even at the deepest level of our hearts. Thank Christ for being cast away from his Father's presence, so that all believers may enjoy that place forever. Ask the Lord to always keep _____'s heart humble and repentant, daily seeking cleansing for sin and the joy of forgiveness.

> Create in me a clean heart, O God,
>   and renew a right spirit within me.
> Cast me not away from your presence,
>   and take not your Holy Spirit from me.
> Restore to me the joy of your salvation,
>   and uphold me with a willing spirit. (Psalm 51:10–12)

_____

_____

_____

_____

_____

_____

SHARING YOUR STORY

Aging is a God-given part of life (Proverbs 20:29). In a few of the previous "Sharing Your Story" sections, you've already reflected on your younger life—related to your work in Proverbs 10, to your life-purpose in 11, and to your recreation in 13. Now consider how you've matured in the area of your thinking. Describe how your opinions, preferences, or tastes are different now than when you were in your twenties, thirties, forties, and later?

_____

_____

_____

_____

_____

Focusing on the recipient of this journal, how have you seen the opinions, tastes, and/or preferences of _____ change over the years—or have they stayed the same?

_____

_____

_____

_____

_____

Proverbs Twenty-One

Guided Tour

The first two verses of chapter 21, along with the last two, serve as bookends for the entire chapter. Their combined message is that no part of life is lived apart from God. He's the undeniable authority of everything—governing (21:1), evaluating (21:2), restraining (21:30), sustaining (21:31)—and everyone is accountable to him (21:2). In light of the Lord's authority and human accountability, the verses in the middle of the chapter (21:3–29) repeatedly remind us that people must be more than wise: they must also be "righteous," conforming to God's ways. (See "Guided Tour" for Proverbs 11.) Men and women must not only fit in wisdom with the patterns of God's world; they must also conform in righteousness to the nature of his revealed character (21:3). And this kind of conforming might communicate that "righteousness" is some super-spiritual, invisible quality. Instead, righteous living displays itself in concrete interactions with the created world. Notice, for example, how you should live righteously in regard to wealth (21:5, 6, 20, 21), housing arrangements (21:9, 19), poverty (21:13, 26), bribery (21:14), justice (21:15), and pleasure (21:17, 21, 25). You must live righteously before the King who will hold you accountable for how you lived in his world. Why? Because your relationship to any aspect of this created world is nothing less than an expression of your relationship to God himself.

AT-A-GLANCE

21:1–2	Bookend: The Lord's Authority in the Real World
21:3–29	Righteous Living in the Real World
21:30–31	Bookend: The Lord's Authority in the Real World

¹ The king's heart in the LORD's hand is a channel of water;
   on all who please him, he turns it.
² Every way of a person may seem upright in his own eyes,
   but the LORD is the one who evaluates hearts.

³ To do righteousness and justice
   is more desirable to the Lord than sacrifice.
⁴ A haughty look and an audacious heart—
   the unplowed field of the wicked—produce sin.
⁵ The calculations of the diligent lead only to profit,
   but everyone who hastens [to get rich] comes only to lack.
⁶ The acquisition of treasures by a lying tongue
   is the windblown breath of those seeking death.
⁷ The violence of wicked people drags them away
   because they refuse to do justice.
⁸ The way of a guilty person is crooked;
   but as for the pure, his deed is straight.
⁹ Better to dwell on a corner of the roof
   than in a house shared with a contentious wife.
¹⁰ A wicked person craves evil;
   his neighbor does not find favor in his eyes.
¹¹ Through fining a mocker, the gullible becomes wise,
   and through paying attention to a wise person he gains knowledge.
¹² The Righteous One is the one who pays attention to the
   household of the wicked person;
   the One who casts down wicked people to calamity.
¹³ As for whoever stops his ear to the cry of the poor,
   indeed, he himself will also cry out and not be answered.
¹⁴ A gift given in secret subdues anger;
   even a bribe in the bosom pacifies strong wrath.
¹⁵ The doing of justice brings joy to the righteous person
   but a terror to those who do iniquity.
¹⁶ A human being who strays from the way of being prudent
   will come to rest in the congregation in the realm of the dead.
¹⁷ The one who loves pleasure is a destitute person;
   the one who loves wine and olive oil will not become rich.
¹⁸ A wicked person is a ransom for the righteous,
   and a treacherous person comes in the place of the upright.
¹⁹ Better to dwell in a desert land
   than to dwell with a contentious and vexing wife.
²⁰ A desirable supply of food and oil are in the dwelling place
   of the wise,
   but a fool gulps his down.
²¹ The one who pursues righteousness and kindness
   will find life, prosperity, and honor.

²² The wise scales the city walls of warriors,
   and pulls down its strong security.
²³ He who guards his mouth and his tongue
   is one who guards his life from distresses.
²⁴ The insolent, presumptuous person—"Mocker is his name"—
   is one who behaves with insolent fury.
²⁵ The craving of the sluggard kills him,
   because his hands refuse to work.
²⁶ All day long he craves greedily,
   but the righteous gives without sparing.
²⁷ The sacrifice of wicked people is an abomination;
   how much more [when] he brings it with evil intent.
²⁸ A false witness will perish,
   but a person who listens well will testify successfully.
²⁹ A wicked man becomes brazen,
   but as for the upright, he discerns his way.

³⁰ There is no wisdom, and there is no understanding,
   and there is no counsel that can stand before the LORD.
³¹ A horse is prepared for the day of war,
   but success belongs to the LORD.

 Reflections

IDENTIFYING A VERSE

Write out the verse that stood out to you from this chapter.

_____

_____

_____

Why did it stand out to you?

_____

_____

_____

GOING DEEPER

According to Proverbs 21:30–31, who is responsible for the outcome of the human endeavor (specifically in this verse it's the human endeavor of warfare)?

_____

_____

Reflect some more on Proverbs 21:30–31. How would you describe the role we as humans have in what we try to accomplish?

_____

_____

Think about your involvement with church or family, and describe one thing you did while depending on the Lord and also being diligent in your responsibilities.

_____

_____

_____

What's been most challenging for you—being dependent or being diligent? Why?

_____

_____

_____

CONNECTING THE GOSPEL

Read Proverbs 21:1 and Acts 2:23. How does the Lord's turning the heart of kings in this verse apply to the crucifixion of Jesus?

_____

_____

What do Isaiah 53:10–11 (below) and Acts 4:27–28 say is the ultimate cause of Jesus's death?

_____

_____

How has the suffering and death of Jesus been turned into the greatest good for God's people (Isaiah 53:11)?

_____

_____

_____

PERSONALIZING A PRAYER

Write out a prayer for yourself and _____ using a portion of Proverbs 21 and Isaiah 53:10–11. Thank God for all the good that Jesus's suffering and death has brought to you and to this world. Ask the Lord to help _____ throughout his/her life both to depend on Jesus's substitutionary death and also to diligently follow his example by taking up his/her cross each day and following him.

> Yet it was the will of the LORD to crush him;
>   he has put him to grief;
> when his soul makes an offering for guilt,
>   he shall see his offspring; he shall prolong his days;
> the will of the LORD shall prosper in his hand.
>   Out of the anguish of his soul he shall see and be satisfied;
> by his knowledge shall the righteous one, my servant,
>   make many to be accounted righteous,
>   and he shall bear their iniquities. (Isaiah 53:10–11)

_____

_____

_____

_____

SHARING YOUR STORY

Living in a large and fancy house carries little enduring value (Proverbs 21:9), while even the smallest home may contain memories that last a lifetime. Give a detailed description of the house and neighborhood in which you lived while growing up. You can include a drawing, if you wish, of your house and neighborhood.

_____

_____

_____

_____

Describe the house, room, and surrounding neighborhood that _____ lived in as a baby, child, and/or teenager.

_____

_____

_____

_____

Proverbs Twenty-Two, Part I

Guided Tour

Proverbs 22:1–16 completes the "proverbs of Solomon" (10:1; 22:17), one of the main sections of Proverbs which started at the beginning of chapter 10. The first sixteen verses of this chapter give primary emphasis to two topics: wealth (22:1–4, 7–9, 16) and words (22:10–14). Secondary topics include both a means for gaining wisdom (i.e., parental discipline, 22:6, 15) and also the consequences for gaining (or alternatively shunning) wisdom (22:3–5).

AT-A-GLANCE

22:1–9	General Focus on Wealth
22:10–16	General Focus on Words

¹ A good name is more desirable than great riches,
   and to be esteemed is better than silver and gold.
² Rich and poor meet together;
   the LORD is the Maker of them all.
³ The shrewd sees evil and hides himself,
   but the gullible pass on and pay the penalty.
⁴ The wage for humility—the fear-of-the-LORD sort—
   is riches, honor, and life.
⁵ Snares, the bird-trap sort, are in the way of the perverse;
   the one who would preserve his life keeps far from them.
⁶ Dedicate a youth according to what his way dictates;
   even when he becomes old, he will not depart from it.
⁷ The rich person rules over poor people,
   and the borrower is a slave to the lender.
⁸ The one who sows injustice will reap empty deception,
   and the rod he wields in his fury will fail.

⁹ As for the generous, he will be blessed
   because he gives from his food to the poor.

¹⁰ Drive out the mocker so that contention might depart,
    and strife and disgrace might cease.
¹¹ As for the one who loves a pure heart,
    whose lips are gracious, the king is a friend of his.
¹² The eyes of the LORD protect knowledge,
    and so he subverts the words of the treacherous.
¹³ The sluggard says, "A lion is outside.
    In the midst of the plaza I will be as good as murdered."
¹⁴ A deep pit is the mouth of the unfaithful wife;
    the one cursed by the LORD falls into it.
¹⁵ Folly is bound up in the youth's heart,
    but the rod of discipline removes it far from him.
¹⁶ He who oppresses the poor to increase [riches] for himself
    [and] he who gives gifts to the rich come only to lack.

 Reflections

IDENTIFYING A VERSE

Write out the verse that stood out to you from this section of chapter 22.

_____

_____

_____

Why did it stand out to you?

_____

_____

_____

_____

GOING DEEPER

Paraphrase Proverbs 22:6 in your own words.

_____

_____

_____

_____

What lessons do you remember being taught as a child, which have stayed with you over the years? Where did you learn them? From whom and how?

_____

_____

_____

_____

List three things you have taught to someone younger. Out of those three, which do you consider the most important? Why?

_____

_____

_____

_____

CONNECTING THE GOSPEL

Read Proverbs 22:9. According to 2 Corinthians 9:6–12, what qualities does God want in those who give to others?

_____

_____

_____

What is the basis and who is the model for your generosity? (See 2 Corinthians 8:9.)

_____

_____

_____

_____

PERSONALIZING A PRAYER

Write out a prayer for yourself and _____ using Proverbs 22:1–16 and 2 Corinthians 9:6–7. Ask the Lord to cultivate a generous heart in _____. Using specific examples, thank the Lord for where you already see _____ living in self-sacrificing, others-serving generosity.

The point is this: whoever sows sparingly will also reap sparingly, and whoever sows bountifully will also reap bountifully. Each one must give as he has decided in his heart, not reluctantly or under compulsion, for God loves a cheerful giver. (2 Corinthians 9:6–7)

_____

_____

_____

_____

SHARING YOUR STORY

As you consider how you were taught as a child (Proverbs 22:6), what values or priorities have stuck with you throughout life?

_____

_____

_____

_____

_____

Which values or priorities have changed? Why?

_____

_____

_____

_____

_____

How do you see _____ living out what she/he has been taught? Use specific examples and stories.

_____

_____

_____

_____

Proverbs Twenty-Two, Part II

Guided Tour

Proverbs 22:17 announces the beginning of a new section in the book with "the sayings of the wise." According to 22:20, thirty individual sayings—some only one verse long (23:9), others up to seven (23:29–35)—comprise this section of Proverbs, which continues until 24:22. Proverbs 22:17–29 contain the first six of the thirty sayings. The first saying (22:17–21) functions similarly to Proverbs 1—9, motivating readers to give their undivided attention to those who teach wisdom. (See "A Bird's-Eye View of Proverbs," page 5, for more on the function of Proverbs 1—9.) The final five sayings in this chapter (and the first five of the next chapter) all feature some kind of negative command ("Do not . . ."), and all but one saying also provide some reason to obey that command. (For the one exception, see 22:28. But the rationale for obeying an identical command is supplied later in 23:10–11.) Finally, note how most of the sayings in this chapter have something to do with the proper (or improper) means of obtaining wealth, prosperity, or success.

AT-A-GLANCE

22:17–21	Saying #1
22:22–23	Saying #2
22:24–25	Saying #3
22:26–27	Saying #4
22:28	Saying #5
22:29	Saying #6

¹⁷ Incline your ear and hear the sayings of the wise,
   and pay attention to to my knowledge,

151

¹⁸ because [it is] lovely when you keep them in your belly,
   [when] they are fixed together on your lips.
¹⁹ In order that your trust may be in the LORD,
   I teach you today, even you!
²⁰ Have I not written for you thirty sayings,
   as advice and knowledge,
²¹ to teach you to be honest in speaking reliable words,
   to bring back reliable reports to those who commission you?

²² Do not rob a poor person because he is a poor,
   and do not crush the afflicted in the gate;
²³ because the LORD will plead their case,
   and so he will despoil those that despoiled them of life.

²⁴ Do not associate with a hothead,
   and with a wrathful person do not get involved;
²⁵ lest you learn his ways,
   and so you fetch a snare for your life.

²⁶ Do not be among those who strike a palm,
   among those who pledge securities for loans.
²⁷ If you do not have the means to repay,
   why should your very bed be taken from under you?

²⁸ Do not move an ancient boundary
   that your ancestors have set.

²⁹ Do you see a person who is skillful in his commission?
   He will present himself before kings;
   he will not present himself before obscure people.

 Reflections

IDENTIFYING A VERSE

Write out the verse that stood out to you from this section of chapter 22.

_____

_____

Why did it stand out to you?

_____

_____

_____

_____

GOING DEEPER

What does Proverbs 22:22 say about mistreating those who are poor?

_____

_____

_____

What warning does 22:26–27 give about assisting others financially?

_____

_____

_____

In your experience, how have you found a wise balance between the instruction given in 22:22 and the one in 22:26–27?

_____

_____

_____

_____

What helpful counsel—about giving to others—would you offer to the person who will receive this journal?

_____

_____

_____

_____

CONNECTING THE GOSPEL

Read Proverbs 22:20–21. What does Proverbs 22:21 say are two reasons God has given us his Word?

_____

_____

_____

What are the four other reasons Paul lists in 2 Timothy 3:16–17 (below)?

_____

_____

_____

The six reasons just listed teach that God's Word is effective in lives. How does Jesus's comment in John 5:39 provide the ultimate reason why God's Word accomplishes its good purposes?

_____

_____

_____

PERSONALIZING A PRAYER

Write out a prayer for yourself and _____ using Proverbs 22:17–29; 2 Timothy 3:16–17; and John 5:39. Ask God to make his Word part of your and _____'s daily life. Thank him for sending his Word to accomplish his good plans in you and _____. Ask the Lord to always open _____'s eyes to see Jesus in the pages of Scripture.

All Scripture is breathed out by God and profitable for teaching, for reproof, for correction, and for training in righteousness, that the man of God may be complete, equipped for every good work. (2 Timothy 3:16–17)

_____

_____

_____

_____

SHARING YOUR STORY

God takes care of his children (Proverbs 22:22–23). How has the Lord met your financial needs over the years? Describe the need, and how he provided for you.

_____

_____

_____

_____

_____

What is the best financial advice you would like to pass on to _____?

_____

_____

_____

_____

_____

Proverbs Twenty-Three

Guided Tour

This chapter includes the next fourteen "Sayings of the Wise." The first five of these sayings in chapter 23 (23:1–11) are similar to the last five of chapter 22. They all do the following:

• Prohibit some kind of bad behavior ("Do not . . ."),

• Provide a rationale for avoiding that behavior, and

• Primarily deal with how to handle material prosperity (22:9 being the exception).

After the first five sayings in this chapter, Sayings #12–20 (Proverbs 23:12–24:2) hang together as the second unit of this chapter. The setting of this unit is the parental training of children (note the occurrences of "my son," "your father," or other family terms in 23:13–15, 18–19, 22, 24–26). The first saying in this unit (#12; Proverbs 23:12) sets the keynote, and, similar to Proverbs 1–9 and 22:17–21, serves to motivate children to give attention to words of wisdom. Proverbs 23:13–14 (Saying #13) speaks to parents about child rearing. Proverbs 23:15–16 and 23:22–25 (Sayings #14 and #17) address children about receiving parental instruction, while Proverbs 23:17–24:2 (Sayings #15–16 and #18–20) warn children about the following kinds of objectionable people or issues: godless sinners (23:17–18), indulgent friends (23:19–21), wayward women (23:26–28), drunkenness (23:29–35), and, in the next chapter, violent troublemakers (24:1–2).

AT-A-GLANCE

23:1–3	Saying #7
23:4–5	Saying #8
23:6–8	Saying #9

23:9	Saying #10
23:10–11	Saying #11
23:12	Saying #12
23:13–14	Saying #13
23:15–16	Saying #14
23:17–18	Saying #15
23:19–21	Saying #16
23:22–25	Saying #17
23:26–28	Saying #18
23:29–35	Saying #19
24:1–2	Saying #20

¹ When you sit down to eat with a ruler,
  mark well what is before you;
² and place a knife in your gullet
  if you are a glutton.
³ do not crave his delicious morsels,
  for that is deceptive food.

⁴ Do not become weary to make yourself rich;
  stop trusting in your own insight.
⁵ Will you let your eyes glance at riches?
  If you do, they are not.
  Surely, without question they will make a set of wings for themselves;
  like an eagle they will fly toward the heavens.

⁶ Do not insist on eating the food of a begrudging host,
  do not even desire his delicious morsels;
⁷ because as he calculates within himself, so is he.
  "Eat and drink," he says to you, but his heart is not with you.
⁸ As for the piece of food that you will have eaten, you will vomit it;
  and you will have wasted your pleasant words.

⁹ In the ears of a fool do not speak,
  because he will show contempt for your prudent words.

¹⁰ Do not move the ancient boundaries;
   and do not enter the fields of the fatherless.

¹¹ Because their Defender is strong,
he will plead their case against you.

¹² Apply your heart to instruction,
your ear to words of knowledge.

¹³ Do not withhold discipline from a youth;
for if your strike him with a rod, he will not die.
¹⁴ You must strike him with a rod
and deliver him from the grave.

¹⁵ My son, if your heart is wise,
my heart will be glad—yes, mine.
¹⁶ And my inward parts will leap for joy
when your lips speak what is upright.

¹⁷ Do not let your heart be envious of sinners,
but be zealous for the fear of the LORD all the time.
¹⁸ Surely there is a latter end;
your hope will not be cut off.

¹⁹ Listen, yes you, my son, and become wise;
direct your heart in the way.
²⁰ Do not be among those who are drunkards,
among those who squander flesh for themselves,
²¹ because drunkards and profligates become destitute,
and drowsiness clothes them in rags.

²² Listen to your father who begot you,
and do not show contempt for your mother when she grows old.
²³ Buy truth and do not sell
wisdom and instruction and insight.
²⁴ The father of a righteous son surely shouts in exultation,
and the one who begets a wise son takes pleasure in him.
²⁵ Let your father and your mother rejoice,
and let the one who bore you shout in exultation.

²⁶ Give to me, my son, your heart,
and let your eyes take pleasure in my ways.
²⁷ Because an unchaste wife is a deep pit,
and the unfaithful woman is a narrow well.

^{28} Indeed, she lays an ambush like a robber,
  and increases the traitors among men.

^{29} Who has "Woe!"? Who has "Alas!"?
  Who has bitter conflicts? Who has complaints?
  Who has bruises needlessly?
  Who has flashing eyes?
^{30} Those who linger over wine,
  those who come to search out jugs of mixed wine.
^{31} Do not look at wine when it is an alluring red,
  when it sparkles in the goblet,
  when it goes down smoothly.
^{32} In the end it will bite like a snake,
  and poison like a viper.
^{33} Your eyes will see incredible sights,
  and your mouth will speak what is perverse.
^{34} And you will become like one sleeping on the high seas,
  like one sleeping on top of the mast.
^{35} "They hit me, but I am not hurt;
  they beat me, but I do not know it.
  When will I wake up
  so that I may continue to seek it yet again?"

24 ^{1} Do not envy evil people,
  and do not crave to be with them;
  ^{2} because their hearts ponder violence,
  and their lips speak malice.

 ## Reflections

IDENTIFYING A VERSE

Write out the verse that stood out to you from chapter 23.

_____

_____

_____

Why did it stand out to you?

_____

_____

_____

_____

GOING DEEPER

How would you paraphrase Proverbs 23:17? Put it in your own words, directed as counsel to the person who will receive this journal.

_____

_____

_____

Read Proverbs 23:18, which is connected to 23:17. Verse 17 is the command to be obeyed, while verse 18 is the incentive or motivation for obeying the command. As you think about this verse and reflect on your own experience, what are some reasons ("hopes") why our hearts tend to envy others?

_____

_____

_____

How do you think that continuing in "the fear of the LORD" (23:17) and having confident "hope" (23:18) can help you address the problem of an envious heart?

_____

_____

_____

From your own life, how have you found help from the Lord to deal with envying others?

_____

_____

_____

_____

CONNECTING THE GOSPEL

Read Proverbs 23:10–11. What characterizes the kind of person who needs the "Defender" (also translated "Redeemer")? (See Exodus 6:6 and Leviticus 25:25–26.)

_____

_____

In 1 Corinthians 1:27–31 (below), how does Paul describe the person who is in need of redemption?

_____

_____

Why would God redeem this kind of person? (See 1 Corinthians 1:31.)

_____

_____

PERSONALIZING A PRAYER

Write out a prayer for yourself and _____ using some portion of Proverbs 23 and 1 Corinthians 1:27–31. Acknowledge before the Lord and _____, your limitations and faults. In light of our sinful tendencies, pray that the Lord would always keep you and _____ aware and humble. Thank the Lord for the various aspects of his salvation mentioned in the passage below. May you and _____ live in light of his glorious goodness and generous grace.

> But God chose what is foolish in the world to shame the wise; God chose what is weak in the world to shame the strong; God chose what is low and despised in the world, even things that are not, to bring to nothing things that are, so that no human being might boast in the presence of God. And because of him you are in Christ Jesus, who became to us wisdom from God, righteousness and sanctification and redemption, so that, as it is written, "Let the one who boasts, boast in the Lord." (1 Corinthians 1:27–31)

_____

_____

_____

_____

SHARING YOUR STORY

Proverbs regularly instructs us to learn from our parents (23:22–25). Whether we listened carefully, we all absorb patterns and traits from the families in which we grew up. List a few of your family's regular routines that you remember from when you were young. What did you like or not like about them?

_____

_____

_____

_____

List a few of your family's special celebrations you remember from when you were young. What did you enjoy about them then?

_____

_____

_____

_____

What do you value now about both the routines and the celebrations?

_____

_____

_____

_____

✒ Proverbs Twenty-Four

Guided Tour

Chapter 24 brings to a conclusion the "Thirty Sayings" (22:20), present-ing the final eleven sayings. With the first two verses serving as the con-clusion to the previous chapter, Proverbs 24:3–14 (Sayings #21–26) form a unit and Proverbs 24:15–22 (Sayings #27–30) another. This chapter's first unit (24:3–14) circles around the wisdom required to succeed—whether in reference to success in general (24:3–4), in adversity (24:5–6, 10–12), or in the future (24:13–14). In contrast to the wisdom necessary for achievement, the plans of the foolish fall short (24:7–9). The second unit in this chapter (24:15–22), returning to the "do not" format (cf. 22:22–24:2), changes from how to interact with success (as in the first unit) to how to deal with evil: do not become evil (24:15–16); do not gloat over evil (24:17–18); do not be anxious over evil (24:19–20); and do not join with evil (24:21–22). To disregard these prohibitions will bring ruin.

After saying #30, Proverbs 24:23–34 presents the next major division of the book: additional "Sayings of the Wise" (24:23). These final twelve verses of this chapter alternate between two pairs of themes: (1) impartial-ity/integrity (24:23–26, 28–29) and (2) poverty/industry (24:27, 30–34).

AT-A-GLANCE

24:1–2	Saying #20 (see previous chapter)
24:3–4	Saying #21
24:5–6	Saying #22
24:7	Saying #23
24:8–9	Saying #24
24:10–12	Saying #25
24:13–14	Saying #26
24:15–16	Saying #27
24:17–18	Saying #28

24:19–20	Saying #29
24:21–22	Saying #30
24:23–34	Additional Sayings of the Wise

[3] By wisdom a household is built,
  and by understanding it is established,
[4] and by knowledge its rooms are filled
  with all kinds of precious and pleasant wealth.

[5] A wise man prevails by might;
  a man of knowledge musters strength.
[6] Surely by guidance you must wage war;
  victory is won through many counselors.

[7] Wisdom is too high for a fool;
  in the gate he must not open his mouth.

[8] As for the one who plans to do evil,
  he will be named "Schemer."
[9] The schemes that come from folly are sin,
  and an abomination to humanity is a mocker.

[10] If you show yourself lax in the time of crisis,
  your strength is meager.
[11] Deliver those being taken to death,
  even hold back those swaying and being led to slaughter.
[12] If you say, "We knew nothing about this,"
  does not even he who weighs motives discern [the truth]?
  As for him who protects your life, does he not know,
  and will he not repay a person according to his conduct?

[13] Eat honey, my son, because it is good,
  and honey from the comb is sweet on your palate;
[14] so know wisdom is like honey for your life.
  If you find wisdom, then there is a blessed future,
  and your hope will not be cut off.

[15] Do not lay an ambush as a wicked person against the dwelling
  place of the righteous,
  do not plunder his resting place;

¹⁶ for if a righteous person falls seven times, then he rises;
  but the wicked stumble in calamity.

¹⁷ When your enemy falls, do not rejoice;
  when he stumbles, do not let your heart shout in exultation;
¹⁸ otherwise the LORD will see,
  and it will be evil in his eyes;
  and he will turn away his wrath from him.

¹⁹ Do not fret because of those who forge evil,
  do not envy the wicked;
²⁰ for the evil person has no blessed future;
  the lamp of the wicked will be snuffed out.

²¹ Fear the LORD, my son, and the king;
  with [intriguing] officials do not get involved.
²² Because disaster from them suddenly appears,
  and who knows what ruin the two of them can inflict?

²³ These also are sayings of the wise.
  To show partiality in giving a verdict is not good.
²⁴ As for anyone who says to the guilty, "You are innocent,"
  peoples will curse him,
  communities will strike him with a curse.
²⁵ As for those who establish what is right, it will be pleasant,
  on them will come a blessing that brings good.
²⁶ He kisses lips—
  the one who gives an honest reply.
²⁷ Establish your out-of-doors work,
  and prepare it in the fields for yourself!
  After [doing that], then build your household!
²⁸ Do not be a witness against your neighbor without reason;
  you would not convince with your lips, would you?
²⁹ Do not say, "As he has done to me, I will do to him;
  I will pay the man back according to his conduct."
³⁰ I passed by the field of the sluggard,
  even the vineyard of a man who lacked sense.
³¹ And behold, the whole of it had grown up as all sorts of nettles,
  its surface was covered over with all kinds of weeds,
  and its stone wall was thrown down.

³² And I saw; I paid attention;
   I observed; I accepted a lesson.
³³ A little sleep, a little slumber,
   a little folding of the arms to lie down,
³⁴ and poverty will come on you like a vagrant,
   and scarcity, like an armed man.

 Reflections

IDENTIFYING A VERSE

Write out the verse that stood out to you from chapter 24.

_____

_____

_____

Why did it stand out to you?

_____

_____

_____

_____

GOING DEEPER

Read 24:27, 30–34. What lessons can you learn from these verses about working diligently and wisely?

_____

_____

_____

_____

Proverbs 24:30–32 provide a personal observation of laziness and irresponsibility, and their consequences. Give some examples of your own (from your life or the lives of others).

_____

_____

_____

What practical advice do you have for _____ about the value of work?

_____

_____

_____

_____

CONNECTING THE GOSPEL

Read Proverbs 24:12. According to this verse (along with Revelation 2:19, 23), who "weighs" the heart and its motives?

_____

_____

_____

What evidence will Jesus use to evaluate your profession of faith in him (Matthew 16:27; 1 Peter 1:17)?

_____

_____

_____

What will reveal, not how worthy you are, but that you belong to the only Worthy One (1 Corinthians 1:7–9, below)?

_____

_____

_____

PERSONALIZING A PRAYER

Write out a prayer for yourself and _____ using parts of Proverbs 24 and 1 Corinthians 1:7–9. Acknowledge where you see God's grace already at work in _____. Pray for _____ that God would do as he promised: sustain his/her faith until the very end. Thank the Lord for his sustaining faithfulness to us, even when we are unfaithful to him. What his grace begins, his grace will finish.

> So that you are not lacking in any gift, as you wait for the revealing of our Lord Jesus Christ, who will sustain you to the end, guiltless in the day of our Lord Jesus Christ. God is faithful, by whom you were called into the fellowship of his Son, Jesus Christ our Lord. (1 Corinthians 1:7–9)

_____

_____

_____

_____

SHARING YOUR STORY

In this life, God's children are not exempt from trouble and difficulty (Proverbs 24:10). Can you describe some of the adversity that you have faced in your life?

_____

_____

_____

_____

As you look back, how did God help you through that hard time?

_____

_____

_____

_____

✒ Proverbs Twenty-Five

Guided Tour

Proverbs 25 begins a five-chapter section (25:1–29:27) which once again features proverbs written by King Solomon, but which were compiled by the men of King Hezekiah (25:1). Whereas the previous "Sayings of the Wise" (Proverbs 22–24) often featured "do not" commands, this section of Solomon's proverbs regularly paints vivid word pictures and employs striking analogies (notice the frequent use of "like" or "as"). Another type of proverb that appears in Proverbs 25–29 is the "too much" proverb, which encourages restraint and balance in life (e.g., 25:16–17, 27).

The first half of chapter 25 (25:2–15) seems to be set in the context of the royal court, where the king makes regal and legal decisions, yet never outside the realm of the true King, the Lord himself (25:2–3). Therefore, all who serve God and king, must handle themselves wisely before such authority. After all, wise (or foolish) living in this context may affect the dynasty (25:4–5), your reputation (25:6–10), and your well-being (25:11–13). The second half of the chapter (framed by two "too much" proverbs about honey, 25:16, 27) takes us from the royal court and brings us closer to home. Solomon offers domestic wisdom mainly for managing conflict: with neighbors (25:16–18), workers (25:19), friends (25:20), enemies (25:21–22), a wife (25:24), messengers (25:25), and the wicked (25:26). The last verse of the chapter begins a section on folly which extends through Proverbs 26:12.

AT-A-GLANCE

25:1	Introduction
25:2–15	Making Decisions in Places of Power
25:16–27	Managing Conflict with People at Home
25:28	(see next chapter)

¹ These also are proverbs of Solomon,
  which the men of Hezekiah the king of Judah copied and collected.

² The glory of God is to hide a matter,
  but the glory of kings is to search out a matter.
³ As for the heavens with reference to height,
  and the earth with reference to depth,
  and the heart of kings, there is no searching out [of them].
⁴ Remove dross from silver,
  and a vessel comes forth for the silversmith.
⁵ Remove a wicked official before a king,
  that his throne may be established by righteousness.
⁶ Do not honor yourself before a king,
  and in the place of great people do not stand.
⁷ Better one says to you, "Come up here,"
  than one humiliate you before a noble.
  What your eyes have seen,
⁸ do not bring hastily to trial,
  lest—what will you do in its end,
  when your peer puts you to shame?
⁹ Plead your case with your peer,
  but do not divulge a confidence,
¹⁰ lest an arbiter will pronounce you guilty,
  and the accusation against you never depart.
¹¹ Apples of gold in a silver sculpture
  are a decision made appropriate to its circumstance.
¹² A gold earring, even an ornament of fine gold,
  is a wise arbiter's rebuke "on" a listening ear.
¹³ Like the coolness of snow at the time of harvest
  is a trustworthy messenger to the one who sends him;
  he refreshes his master.
¹⁴ Clouds and wind and no rain
  is a man who boasts of a gift he does not give.
¹⁵ Through patience a ruler is persuaded,
  and a soft tongue shatters a bone.

¹⁶ [If] you have found honey, eat what you require,
  lest you have more than enough of it and vomit it.
¹⁷ Make your foot scarce [and turn away] from your neighbor's house,

lest he have more than enough of you and hate you.
 ¹⁸ A war club, or a sword, or a sharpened arrow
    is a man who testifies against his neighbor as a false witness.
 ¹⁹ A decaying tooth or a turned foot
    is reliance on a treacherous person in the time of adversity.
 ²⁰ One who puts off a garment on a cold day,
    [one who pours] vinegar on a wound,
    [is] one who sings songs to a heavy heart.
 ²¹ If the one who hates you is hungry, give him food to eat,
    and if he is thirsty, give him water to drink.
 ²² For burning coals you are taking [and heaping] on his head,
    and the LORD will repay you.
 ²³ Like a north wind that brings forth rain,
    a sly tongue [brings] a face struck by a curse.
 ²⁴ Better is dwelling on a corner of a roof
    than "in" a house shared with a contentious wife.
 ²⁵ Cold water to a weary person
    and a good report from a distant land.
 ²⁶ A muddied spring, a ruined fountain,
    [is] a righteous person who sways before the wicked.
 ²⁷ To eat honey excessively is not good;
    nor is it honorable to search out weighty matters.

 Reflections

IDENTIFYING A VERSE

Write out the verse that stood out to you from chapter 25.

_____

_____

Why did it stand out to you?

_____

_____

_____

GOING DEEPER

Read Proverbs 25:13. In what ways is a "trustworthy messenger" like "coolness of snow" in a warm season of the year?

_____

_____

_____

Read Proverbs 25:19. In what ways is a "treacherous [unfaithful] person" like a "decaying tooth" or twisted ankle?

_____

_____

_____

Where in your life experiences have you seen the refreshment brought by a reliable person and/or the pain brought by an unreliable one? Especially describe the refreshment or pain that was brought by the person.

_____

_____

_____

_____

Reflect and share what has motivated you to try to be a faithful and reliable person, employee, family member, and Christian.

_____

_____

_____

_____

CONNECTING THE GOSPEL

Read Proverbs 25:21–22. How did Jesus obey the wise instruction of Proverbs 25:21–22 (1 Peter 2:23)?

_____

_____

_____

Why did Jesus obey this command (1 Peter 2:24–25)?

_____

_____

_____

PERSONALIZING A PRAYER

Write out a prayer for yourself and _____ using Proverbs 25:21–22 and 1 Peter 2:23–24. As you review this passage (below), give thanks to the Lord for all it cost him to purchase our salvation. Pray for the Lord to help _____ to live according to the example set by our Lord. Ask him to enable _____, when he/she strays, to rely on the Lord's sacrifice as the complete payment for sin and to confidently return to the welcome of his fold.

> When he was reviled, he did not revile in return; when he suffered, he did not threaten, but continued entrusting himself to him who judges justly. He himself bore our sins in his body on the tree, that we might die to sin and live to righteousness. By his wounds you have been healed. _For you were straying like sheep, but have now returned to the Shepherd and Overseer of your souls._ (1 Peter 2:23–25, emphasis mine)

_____

_____

_____

_____

_____

SHARING YOUR STORY

Solomon wrote and read a lot, and his learning helped many people during his lifetime and still today (Proverbs 25:1; 1 Kings 4:29–34). Use the table below to make a list of the five books that have been most influential in your life.

In the second column add a brief explanation of why they are important to you.

In the third column describe how you discovered them.

Title	Explanation	Discovered?

✒ Proverbs Twenty-Six

Guided Tour

This chapter, like the previous one, features both dramatic mini-stories (e.g., 26:13, 15, 27) and comparison words ("like" or "as," indicating the use of a simile). Solomon continues to employ these real-life illustrations and examples in order to bring the reader face-to-face with the ugliness of folly and so unmask its potential appeal. After an introduction, which warns against the dangers of an undisciplined person (25:28), the first section of this chapter (26:1–12) shines the spotlight more specifically on the "fool"—what a fool is like and what he deserves. The rest of the chapter presents profiles of the following unsavory characters: the sluggard (26:13–16), the meddling prankster (26:17–19), the gossip (26:20–22), and the hostile liar (26:23–28).

AT-A-GLANCE

25:28	Introductory Warning
26:1–12	The Fool
26:13–16	The Sluggard
26:17–19	The Prankster
26:20–22	The Gossip
26:23–28	The Liar

25 ²⁸ A breached city, which has no wall,
    a person whose spirit has no restraint.

26 ¹ As snow in summer and rain in harvest,
    so honor is not fitting for a fool.
  ² As a fluttering bird, as a flying sparrow,
    so an undeserved curse does not come to pass.
  ³ A whip for a warhorse, a bit for a donkey,
    and a rod for backs of fools.

⁴ Do not answer a fool according to his folly,
  lest you become like him—even you!
⁵ Answer a fool according to his folly,
  lest he become wise in his own eyes.
⁶ One who chops off [his] feet, who drinks violence,
  is one who sends messages by the hand of a fool.
⁷ Legs dangle from a cripple,
  and a proverb dangles in the mouth of fools.
⁸ Like one who binds a stone in a sling
  is the person who gives honor to a fool.
⁹ A thornbush in the hand of a drunkard,
  and a proverb in the mouth of a fool.
¹⁰ An archer who pierces every passer-by,
  and one who hires a fool, and one who hires those who pass by.
¹¹ As a dog returns to its vomit,
  so a fool repeats his folly.
¹² Do you see a person who is wise in his own eyes?
  There is more hope for a fool than for him.

¹³ A sluggard says, "A [fierce] lion is in the way,
  a lion is in the plaza!"
¹⁴ A door turns on its pivot,
  and a sluggard on his couch.
¹⁵ A sluggard buries his hand in a pan;
  he is too weary to return it to his mouth.
¹⁶ A sluggard is wiser in his own eyes
  than seven men who give a judicious answer.

¹⁷ One who grabs the ears of a dog passing by
  is one who becomes enraged in a dispute not his own.
¹⁸ Like a madman who shoots
  flaming missiles and deadly arrows,
¹⁹ so is a person who deceives his neighbor
  and says, "Am I not only joking?"

²⁰ Without wood a fire goes out;
  and when there is no slanderer, a conflict calms down.
²¹ Glowing charcoal to embers and wood to fire,
  and a contentious person to kindling strife.
²² The words of a slanderer are like tidbits;
  so they descend into one's innermost being.

²³ Silver dross glazed over a potsherd
   is smooth lips and an evil heart.
²⁴ With his lips an enemy dissembles,
   and in his inner being he harbors deception.
²⁵ If he makes his voice charming, do not trust him,
   for seven abominations are in his heart.
²⁶ His hatred is concealed by deception;
   his evil is revealed in a congregation.
²⁷ As for the one who digs a pit, he will fall into it;
   as for the one who rolls a stone, it will return to him.
²⁸ The lying tongue hates those oppressed by it,
   but the smooth mouth works ruin.

 Reflections

IDENTIFYING A VERSE

Write out the verse that stood out to you from chapter 26.

_____

_____

_____

Why did it stand out to you?

_____

_____

_____

GOING DEEPER

Proverbs 26:4 directs you to "answer not a fool according to [in the same way as] his folly." Why do you think it would be foolish to trade insults with a fool?

_____

_____

_____

_____

Proverbs 26:5 instructs you to "answer a fool according to [in light of] his folly." If a fool's folly isn't addressed and exposed for what it is, what do you think might result?

_____

_____

_____

Knowing how to speak wisely to a fool takes skill. Reread 26:17–28, then make a list of the advice that these verses give on what wise speech to a fool might sound like.

_____

_____

_____

What advice would you give to _____ about how and how not to speak to a fool? In your experience, what have you found to be effective (or not effective)?

_____

_____

_____

_____

CONNECTING THE GOSPEL

Read Proverbs 26:12, 16. In what specific ways does Romans 12:9–21 concretely encourage a life that's both wise and also overflowing with love?

_____

_____

_____

Compare Proverbs 26:12, 16 with Romans 12:16 (below), and Proverbs 26:13–16 with Romans 12:11. What similarities do you notice? What are the differences?

_____

_____

_____

In what ways did Jesus live out for us the wisdom and love discussed in Romans 12:9–21 (see especially 12:17, 20–21).

_____

_____

_____

PERSONALIZING A PRAYER

Write out a prayer for yourself and _____ using some portion of Proverbs 26 and Romans 12:16. Thank Christ for his humility in coming to earth to live and die for others. Ask him to help you and _____ mirror his example in your words, actions, and attitudes.

> Live in harmony with one another. Do not be haughty, but associate with the lowly. Never be wise in your own sight. (Romans 12:16)

_____

_____

_____

_____

SHARING YOUR STORY

Proverbs 26:6 reminds us that unreliable people make life difficult. In contrast, list three people that you thoroughly depend on.

_____

_____

_____

_____

How did you come to rely on them?

_____

_____

_____

_____

What are the most important characteristics for someone you are relying on to have?

_____

_____

_____

_____

Proverbs Twenty-Seven

Guided Tour

Instead of talking about people you need to avoid (as in chapter 26), most of chapter 27 focuses on various positive relationships within the circles of friends and family. Humility, the key to any healthy relationship, sets the overall tone (by negative example in 27:1 and positive example in 27:2). The rest of the chapter divides into three sections, each emphasizing some aspect of relationships: conflict (27:3–10); discernment (11–22); and authority (see comment on 27:23–27 below). Throughout the first 18 verses, Solomon sketches a variety of behaviors that identify true friendship (27:5–6, 9, 17) or its opposite (27:3–4, 10, 13–14), before providing practical advice for how to evaluate the actual nature of a friend (27:19–22). Additionally, the close connections of family also receive attention in this chapter (parents in 27:11–12; a wife in 27:15–16; and servants in 27:18), with special emphasis on the virtues of keeping these relationships close (27:8, 10). The final five verses of this chapter extend the discussion of a rural household by giving instruction about caring for animals on the family farm (27:23–27), which also seems to function as a metaphor describing wise living for those who wield authority (see 27:24). As you read, notice the logical flow of thought which runs through and unites these last five verses.

AT-A-GLANCE

27:1–2	Humility and Relationships
27:3–10	Conflict and Relationships
27:11–22	Discernment and Relationship
27:23–27	Authority and Relationships

¹ Do not boast about tomorrow,
   for you do not know what a day may bring forth.
² Let a stranger and not your own mouth praise you,
   an outsider, and let not your own lips praise you.

³ The weight of a stone and the burden of sand—
  but the vexation of a fool is heavier than both.
⁴ The cruelty of wrath and the torrents of anger—
  but who can stand before jealousy?
⁵ Open rebuke is better than concealed love.
⁶ The wounds of a friend are faithful,
  but the kisses of an enemy are too excessive.
⁷ A sated person tramples down a honeycomb,
  but as for a hungry person, every bitter thing is sweet.
⁸ Like a bird that flees from its nest,
  so is a person who flees from his home.
⁹ Olive oil and incense make the heart glad,
  and the sweetness of one's friend comes from passionate counsel.
¹⁰ Your friend and your father's friend do not forsake,
  and the house of your relative do not enter in the time of distress.
  A close, next-door neighbor is better than a relative who is far off.

¹¹ Be wise, my son, and make my heart glad,
  so that I might answer him who reproaches me.
¹² A shrewd person, who sees evil, hides himself;
  the gullible, who pass on, are fined.
¹³ Take away his garment when one becomes surety for a stranger;
  and for a foreign woman impound it.
¹⁴ As for the one who blesses his neighbor with a loud voice early in
  the morning,
  it will be reckoned to him as a curse.
¹⁵ A leaky roof in a cloudburst
  and a contentious wife are alike.
¹⁶ Those who shelter her shelter wind,
  and oil meets his right hand.
¹⁷ Iron is sharpened with iron,
  and a person sharpens the face of his friend.
¹⁸ He who protects a fig tree will eat its fruit,
  and he who guards his master will be honored.
¹⁹ As, looking in water, a face looks to a face,
  so a human being's heart looks to a human being.
²⁰ The Grave and Abaddon are never satisfied,
  and the eyes of humankind are never satisfied.
²¹ The crucible is for silver and the furnace for gold,
  and a person is tested according to his praise.

²² If you grind a fool in a mortar, in the midst of groats with a pestle,
    his folly will not depart from him.

²³ Be sure you know the condition of your flocks,
    pay attention to [your] herds.
²⁴ Wealth does not endure forever,
    and certainly not a crown from generation to generation.
²⁵ If the grass is removed, then the new growth appears;
    and if the vegetation of the mountains is harvested,
²⁶ the young rams will provide your clothing,
    and your he-goats, the price of a field.
²⁷ And you will have enough goats' milk
    for your food, for the food of your household,
    and for the life of your servant girls.

 Reflections

IDENTIFYING A VERSE

Write out the verse that stood out to you from chapter 27.

_____

_____

_____

Why did it stand out to you?

_____

_____

_____

_____

GOING DEEPER

Read Proverbs 27:19. How is your life like a mirror ("water")? And given the nature of the human heart, why is this helpful?

_____

_____

_____

_____

The next three verses (vv. 20–22) focus on three areas of life that may especially reveal what is in the heart: how you handle your desires (27:20), praise (27:21), and correction (27:22). In your own words, identify what verses 20–22 say about these three areas of life.

_____

_____

_____

_____

Why do you think these three areas of life (desires, praise, and correction) especially reveal what we love and value?

_____

_____

_____

_____

As you have more clearly understood your heart over the years (perhaps through these three areas), how has this discovery affected you? What have been your initial responses? Then how has the Lord led you to respond differently?

_____

_____

_____

_____

CONNECTING THE GOSPEL

Read Proverbs 27:20 and 1 John 2:15–17 (below). How does the 1 John passage elaborate on Proverbs 27:20?

_____

_____

_____

As an approach for defeating evil desires, what was Moses's mental strategy and heart posture recorded in Hebrews 11:24–26?

_____

_____

_____

PERSONALIZING A PRAYER

Write out a prayer for yourself and _____ using Proverbs 27 and 1 John 2:15–17. Take a moment to pray about the desires you have that are taking you in the wrong direction. Pray for _____ that his/her deepest desire will be to love God more than anything or anyone.

> Do not love the world or the things in the world. If anyone loves the world, the love of the Father is not in him. For all that is in the world—the desires of the flesh and the desires of the eyes and pride of life is not from the Father but is from the world. And the world is passing away along with its desires, but whoever does the will of God abides forever. (1 John 2:15–17)

_____

_____

_____

_____

_____

SHARING YOUR STORY

No person can accurately predict the future (Proverbs 27:1). How has your life turned out differently than you had planned?

_____

_____

_____

_____

Which of those changes in plan are you thankful for?

_____

_____

_____

_____

What are your hopes for the future for _____?

_____

_____

_____

_____

What advice can you share about how to remain thankful even when plans change unexpectedly?

_____

_____

_____

_____

✒ Proverbs Twenty-Eight

Guided Tour

Chapters 28 and 29 share many of the same themes. They both contain common topics (righteousness/wickedness, wealth/poverty, and kings/rulers) and a similar style (many two-line "antithetical" proverbs, in which the second line supplies a contrast to the first). The chapter divides into two main sections 28:1–11 and 28:12–28. Both halves speak often about temptations related to money: the temptation both to chase what you covet and also to abuse what you have. An additional theme of the first section (28:1–11) is spiritual blindness, which stands in contrast to knowledge and discernment. Foolish and wicked people are deluded (28:1–5, 7–11) often through wealth and prosperity (28:6, 8, 11). The main second section (28:12–28), bookended by matching verses (28:12, 28), addresses a person's evil and guilt and how these affect others. Specifically, notice the repeated (and often unsavory) interaction between people and: God (28:13–14, 25), rulers (28:12, 15, 16, 28), victims (28:17, 21, 25, 27), friends (28:23), and parents (28:24). The first verse of the next chapter serves as a fitting conclusion to both the first and second sections of this chapter: persistence in spiritual blindness (correlating to 28:1–11) means remaining in sin (28:12–28) which ultimately will lead to ruinous consequences.

AT-A-GLANCE

28:1–11	Money and Spiritual Blindness
28:12–28	Money and Personal Interactions
29:1	Conclusion

¹ The wicked flee, though no one is pursuing,
  but the righteous are confident like a lion.
² Because of the transgression of a land, its princes are many;
  but because of a discerning person, one who knows,

what is right endures.

³ A destitute man and one who oppresses the poor—
  a rain that washes away and there is no food.
⁴ Those who abandon instruction praise the wicked,
  but those who keep instruction strive against them.
⁵ Evil people do not discern what is right,
  but the one who seeks the Lord discerns everything.
⁶ Better a destitute person who walks in his integrity,
  than [one who walks in] the crookedness of double-dealing
  ways, though he is rich.
⁷ A discerning son guards instruction,
  but one who associates with profligates puts his father to shame.
⁸ The one who increases his wealth by taking interest of any sort
  from the poor
  gathers it for one who is gracious to the poor.
⁹ As for one who turns his ear aside from hearing instruction—
  even his prayer is detestable.
¹⁰ As for one who misleads the upright into an evil way—
  he will fall into his own pit;
  but the blameless will inherit good things.
¹¹ A rich person is wise in his own eyes,
  but a discerning poor person searches him out.

¹² When the righteous triumph, the splendor is great,
  but when the wicked rise up, mortals must be searched out.
¹³ The one who conceals his transgressions will not succeed,
  but the one who confesses and abandons them will obtain mercy.
¹⁴ Blessed is the person who trembles [before the Lord] continually;
  but the one who hardens his heart will fall in calamity.
¹⁵ A roaring lion and a ravenous, charging bear
  is a wicked ruler over a poor people.
¹⁶ A leader who is lacking in understanding multiplies extortion;
  those who hate ill-gotten gain prolong days.
¹⁷ A mortal oppressed by shedding the blood of life
  will flee to the pit. Let no one restrain him.
¹⁸ The one who walks as a blameless person will be helped,
  but the double-dealing crook will fall into a pit.
¹⁹ The one who works his land is filled with food,
  but the one who pursues worthless ventures is filled with poverty.

²⁰ A conscientious person abounds in blessings,
   but one who hastens to get rich will not escape punishment.
²¹ To show partiality is not good;
   even for a portion of food a man may commit a crime.
²² The miser is hasty for wealth,
   but he does not know that poverty will come to him.
²³ The one who reprimands a mortal about his conduct finds favor,
   not the deceptive flatterer.
²⁴ The one who robs his father and his mother while saying,
   "There is no crime"—he is a companion to a person who destroys.
²⁵ The unrestrained appetite stirs up strife,
   but the one who trusts in the LORD will be fattened.
²⁶ The one who trusts in his own heart—he is a fool;
   but the one who walks in wisdom—he will be delivered.
²⁷ As for the one who gives to the poor, there is no lack;
   but the one who shuts his eyes abounds in curses.
²⁸ When the wicked rise up, mortals hide themselves;
   but when they perish, the righteous thrive.

29 ¹ As for a person often reproved [and] who hardens his neck,
   in an instant he will be broken, and without a remedy.

 Reflections

IDENTIFYING A VERSE

Write out the verse that stood out to you from chapter 28.

_____

_____

_____

Why did it stand out to you?

_____

_____

_____

GOING DEEPER

What negative consequences await those who pursue riches at any cost? (See Proverbs 28:8, 20, 22, 27.)

_____

_____

_____

_____

Why would someone pursue riches despite the negative consequences? According to Proverbs 28:11, what is true of this kind of person?

_____

_____

_____

_____

What blessings are in store for the person who acquires and manages wealth honestly, wisely, and generously? (See Proverbs 28:8, 16, 19–20, 27.)

_____

_____

_____

_____

How have you seen the Lord provide for you and/or your family over the years? Share at least two examples of God's providing for you.

_____

_____

_____

_____

_____

_____

_____

CONNECTING THE GOSPEL

Read Proverbs 28:13 and 1 John 1:5–10. According to these two passages, why do we receive cleansing and mercy when we confess our sins? List all the reasons you identify in these verses.

_____

_____

_____

_____

_____

PERSONALIZING A PRAYER

Write out a prayer for yourself and _____ using Proverbs 28 and 1 John 1:5–10 (below). Take a moment to pray and ask for forgiveness and mercy for specific sins. Thank God that he promises to cleanse us from all unrighteousness. Pray for _____ that he/she will daily acknowledge his/her sin and ask for forgiveness.

> This is the message we have heard from him and proclaim to you, that God is light, and in him is no darkness at all. If we say we have fellowship with him while we walk in darkness, we lie and do not practice the truth. But if we walk in the light, as he is in the light, we have fellowship with one another, and the blood of Jesus his Son cleanses us from all sin. If we say we have no sin, we deceive ourselves, and the truth is not in us. If we confess our sins, he is faithful and just to forgive us our sins and to cleanse us from all unrighteousness. If we say we have not sinned, we make him a liar, and his word is not in us. (1 John 1:5–10)

_____

_____

_____

_____

_____

SHARING YOUR STORY

The Lord encourages generosity as a way to help others (Proverbs 28:27). As you've benefited from someone else's generosity, what is the most meaningful gift (or gifts) that you have received?

_____

_____

_____

_____

Why is it meaningful to you? What's the story behind this gift?

_____

_____

_____

_____

Have you ever lost something that was meaningful to you? How did that happen? Was it ever found?

_____

_____

_____

_____

✒ Proverbs Twenty-Nine

Guided Tour

Chapter 29 is the last chapter in the second main collection of proverbs by Solomon (25:1–29:27). The chapter breaks into two sections (29:2–15 and 29:16–27) both of which begin with a similar verse (29:2; 29:16). After verse 1, which serves as the conclusion to chapter 28, the first section (29:2–15) repeatedly deals with the topic of oppression. In addition to personally experiencing "self-inflicted oppression" due to sinful choices (29:3, 5–6), the following people also know the sting of maltreatment: citizens (29:2, 4, 8, 12), the poor (29:7, 13–14), and the upright (29:10). Two verses (29:3, 15) in this first section highlight the value of parental discipline. Parents should discipline their children in order to prevent them from oppressing others when they become adults. Yet these two key verses raise a question: How does rearing children lead to the desired outcomes? The second section of this chapter (29:16–27) provides answers to this question. Children find their sinful ways corrected through discipline (29:17, 19), God's revealed truth (29:18), humility (29:23), and trust in the Lord (29:25–26). By contrast, people resist correction (and therefore encounter bad consequences) by being quick to talk (29:20), pampered (29:21), quick-tempered (29:22), proud (29:23), friends with criminals (29:24), and ensnared by the fear of man (29:25).

AT-A-GLANCE

29:1	(see previous chapter)
29:2–15	The Problem of Oppression
29:16–27	The Answer of Correction

² When the righteous thrive, the people rejoice;
  but when a wicked person rules, people groan.
³ A person who loves wisdom makes his father glad,
  but one who associates with prostitutes squanders [his] wealth.

⁴ A king through justice establishes a land;
  but whoever exacts "contributions" or gives them tears it down.
⁵ A man who flatters his neighbor
  is one who spreads a net for his feet.
⁶ In the transgression of an evil person is a snare,
  but the righteous person shouts for joy and is glad.
⁷ A righteous person is one who knows court decisions for the poor,
  but a wicked person does not understand knowing.
⁸ Mockers cause a city to pour forth anger,
  but wise people turn back anger.
⁹ If a wise person confronts the fool in court,
  [the fool] rages and scoffs, and there is no calm.
¹⁰ Bloodthirsty people hate the person of integrity;
  and as for the upright, they seek to kill each of them.
¹¹ A fool gives full vent to his rage,
  but the wise finally stills it.
¹² As for a ruler who pays attention to deceptive words,
  all his attendants become wicked.
¹³ Poor and oppressor meet together;
  the LORD is the one who gives light to the eyes of both.
¹⁴ As for a king who judges the poor through truth,
  his throne is established forever.
¹⁵ A rod and reproof give wisdom,
  but an undisciplined youth brings his mother shame.

¹⁶ When the wicked thrive, transgression abounds;
  but the righteous will gaze on their downfall.
¹⁷ Discipline your son so that he will give you rest,
  and he will give delight to you.
¹⁸ Without a revelation the people fall into anarchy,
  but as for the one who carefully obeys the teaching, blessed is he!
¹⁹ A slave is not disciplined by words;
  though he understands, he does not respond.
²⁰ Do you see a person who is hasty with his words?
  [There is] more hope for a fool than for him.
²¹ [If] one pampers his slave from youth,
  afterward he will be insolent.
²² A hothead stirs up strife;
  a wrathful person is one who abounds in transgressions.

²³ The pride of a mortal will bring him low,
  but the lowly in spirit will lay hold of honor.
²⁴ Whoever is an accomplice with a thief hates his life;
  he hears the divine curse, but will not testify.
²⁵ Panic induced by a mortal lays a snare,
  but the one who trusts in the LORD will be protected.
²⁶ Many are they who seek the face of a ruler,
  but justice for an individual comes from the LORD.
²⁷ An unjust person is an abomination to the righteous,
  but the upright in his way is an abomination to the wicked.

 ## Reflections

IDENTIFYING A VERSE

Write out the verse that stood out to you from chapter 29.

_____

_____

_____

Why did it stand out to you?

_____

_____

_____

GOING DEEPER

If living in the "fear of the LORD" means that you have an awareness of God, that he is big and you are not, what might it mean to live in fear of other people (Proverbs 29:25)?

_____

_____

_____

What are some reasons why people fear other people? What might they be afraid will be done to them, or that they might lose?

_____

_____

_____

What is the contrast and antidote to living in the fear of man ("panic induced by a mortal") (Proverbs 29:25)?

_____

_____

_____

How does having confidence in the LORD provide the remedy for being controlled by your fears of people?

_____

_____

_____

Share a time when you were afraid of people and the Lord helped you? What did his help look and sound like?

_____

_____

_____

CONNECTING THE GOSPEL

Read Proverbs 29:3 and Luke 15:11–19. Based on Proverbs 29:3, how might you expect the father in Luke 15 to respond?

_____

_____

How does the father in the parable of Luke 15:20–24 (below) actually respond?

_____

_____

_____

Since the father in the parable represents our heavenly Father, how does his response give you hope?

_____

_____

_____

PERSONALIZING A PRAYER

Write out a prayer for yourself and _____ using Proverbs 29 and Luke 15:20–24. Thank your heavenly Father that he welcomes those who repent. Pray for _____ that he/she will know the Father's great love for him/her, regardless of whether he/she at any moment is a rule-keeper or rule-breaker.

> "And he arose and came to his father. But while he was still a long way off, his father saw him and felt compassion, and ran and embraced him and kissed him. And the son said to him, 'Father, I have sinned against heaven and before you. I am no longer worthy to be called your son.' But the father said to his servant, 'Bring quickly the best robe, and put it on him, and put a ring on his hand, and shoes on his feet. And bring the fattened calf and kill it, and let us eat and celebrate. For this my son was dead, and is alive again; he was lost, and is found.' And they began to celebrate." (Luke 15:20–24)

_____

_____

_____

SHARING YOUR STORY

Proverbs 29 says much about parents and children. What advice from your parents do you wish you had paid better attention to? Why?

_____

_____

_____

_____

_____

List two pieces of advice you want _____ to remember for rearing his/her own children.

_____

_____

_____

_____

_____

✒ Proverbs Thirty

Guided Tour

Chapter 30 begins the next major division within the book of Proverbs: the "sayings of Agur" (30:1). Agur apparently was numerically inclined. Notice how all through this chapter he employs numbers and groupings of observations to masterfully craft a cumulative point (cf. 30:7, 15–16, 18–20, 21–23, 24–28, 29–31). Verses 1–6, which is Agur's personal introduction to the entire chapter, feature a humble confession, affirming personal inadequacy and scriptural sufficiency. Verses 7–9 then set the keynote theme for the rest of the chapter, which is all about greedy and arrogant ambition. In attempting to get ahead (or in retaliation for not getting ahead), people must not speak evil against servants (30:10) or parents (30:11–14). Indeed, this kind of selfish ambition will never yield true satisfaction (30:15–16) nor escape punishment (30:17). Verses 18–31 continue this treatment of ambition through four sub-units, each of which features a numerical sequence and reiterates the truth that we need to live within God-given limits. The first section (30:18–20) communicates: Don't pursue a woman who is not your own. The second section (30:21–23) climaxes with the message: Don't pursue a position not your own. The third section (30:24–28) makes the point: Don't be discontent with or neglect to utilize the little advantages you have. And the fourth section (30:29–33) gives the reminder: Don't seek to exalt yourself over those in power.

AT-A-GLANCE

30:1–6	Personal Introduction
30:7–9	Prayers for Contentment
30:10–17	Warnings against Ambitious Speech
30:18–33	Case Studies of Ambition Pursuits

¹ The sayings of Agur son of Jakeh. An oracle.
The inspired utterance of the man to Ithiel:
"I am weary, O God, but I can prevail.

² Surely I am too stupid to be a man;
   indeed, I do not have the understanding of a human being.
³ Indeed, I have not learned wisdom,
   but I want to experience the knowledge of the Holy One.
⁴ Who has ever ascended to heaven and come down?
   Who has ever gathered up the wind in his fists?
   Who has ever wrapped up the waters in his robe?
   Who has established all the ends of the earth?
   What is his name? And what is his son's name?
   Surely you know!
⁵ Every word of God is purified;
   he is a shield to those who take refuge in him.
⁶ Do not add to his word,
   lest he convict you and you be proved a liar.

⁷ Two things I ask of you;
   do not withhold [them] from me before I die.
⁸ A deceitful lie keep far away from me.
   Poverty or riches do not give me.
   Provide me my quota of food;
⁹ lest I be sated and dissemble and say, "Who is the LORD?"
   or lest I become poor and I steal,
   and so do violence to the name of my God.

¹⁰ Do not slander a slave to his master,
   lest he curse you, and you become liable.
¹¹ A generation—they curse their fathers
   and do not bless their mothers.
¹² A generation—[they are] pure in their own eyes,
   but are not cleansed from their excrement.
¹³ A generation—how they raise their eyes!
   And [how] they lift up their pupils!
¹⁴ A generation—their teeth are swords
   and their jawbones are butcher knives
   to devour the poor [and eliminate] them from the earth,
   and the needy from humanity.
¹⁵ The horse leech has two daughters: "Give!" "Give!"
   They are three things that are never satisfied,
   four that never say, "Enough!"

¹⁶ Sheol and the barren womb,
  the land that is never satisfied with water,
  and fire that never says, "Enough!"
¹⁷ As for the eye that mocks a father and shows contempt for the gray hair of a mother,
  the ravens of the wadi will peck it out,
  and the vultures will devour it.

¹⁸ They are three things that are too wonderful for me;
  and as for four, I do not know them:
¹⁹ the way of an eagle in the sky, the way of a serpent on a rock.
  the way of a ship in the heart of the sea,
  and the way of a man with a virgin.
²⁰ Thus is the way of an adulteress:
  she eats and wipes her mouth, and says: "I have not done iniquity."
²¹ Under three things the earth trembles,
  under four it cannot endure:
²² under an official when he becomes king,
  and an outcast when he becomes full of food;
²³ under a hated woman when she gets married,
  and a maidservant when she dispossesses her mistress.
²⁴ As for four things, they are small creatures of the earth,
  but they are extremely wise:
²⁵ ants are a people without strength,
  and so they store up their food in the harvest.
²⁶ Rock badgers are a people without numerical strength,
  and so they place their houses in the rocks.
²⁷ Locusts have no king,
  and so all of them go forth dividing into companies.
²⁸ A wall lizard you can catch with two hands,
  but it lives in the king's palace.
²⁹ They are three creatures that excel in their stride,
  and four that excel in their movement:
³⁰ the lion is a hero among animals,
  and does not turn back from the face of anything;
³¹ the strutting rooster or the he-goat,
  and a king no one dares to resist.
³² If you will play the fool in exalting yourself,
  and if you scheme to do so, clap your hand over your mouth,

³³ for [as] the churning of cream produces butter,
    and as the wringing of the nose produces blood,
    so the "pressing out" of wrath produces strife.

 Reflections

IDENTIFYING A VERSE

Write out the verse that stood out to you from chapter 30.

_____

_____

_____

Why did it stand out to you?

_____

_____

_____

_____

GOING DEEPER

What "two things" (Proverbs 30:7) are requested in Proverbs 30:8a and 8b?

_____

_____

_____

Focusing on the second of the "two things," what examples of 30:8b, are given in the form of a prayer in 30:8c–9? In your own words, what does "give me neither poverty nor riches" look like?

_____

_____

_____

What, according to Proverbs 30:9, might happen if you were satisfied
("sated") with prosperity? And what might happen if you were over-
whelmed with poverty? In both of these, what lies at the deepest heart
of the concern?

_____

_____

_____

_____

_____

If Proverbs 30:9 presents possible negative outcomes, how might you
restate this verse positively? What should our response be when enjoying
abundance or when experiencing need?

_____

_____

_____

_____

Share examples of what the Lord has taught you about thankfulness and
contentment in your life.

_____

_____

_____

_____

CONNECTING THE GOSPEL

Read Proverbs 30:3–4 and John 3:9–15 (below). Has any human being ever risen to the challenge of Proverbs 30:4 and been able to ascend to heaven and drink pure wisdom from its source? What does John 3:9–15 teach about the only successful ascent and how you may benefit from it?

_____

_____

_____

_____

PERSONALIZING A PRAYER

Write out a prayer for yourself and _____ using parts of Proverbs 30 and John 3:9–15. In your prayer reflect on how much bigger God is than you (cf. Proverbs 30:1–4). Give praise for Jesus's willingness to leave the perfections of heaven (its wisdom, beauty, glory) and embrace the imperfections of earth (its folly, pain, and sin). Thank God for Jesus being lifted up on the cross and pray for _____ that he/she will believe in Jesus and have eternal life.

> Nicodemus said to him, "How can these things be?" Jesus answered him, "Are you the teacher of Israel and yet you do not understand these things? Truly, truly, I say to you, we speak of what we know, and bear witness to what we have seen, but you do not receive our testimony. If I have told you earthly things and you do not believe, how can you believe if I tell you heavenly things? No one has ascended into heaven except he who descended from heaven, the Son of Man. And as Moses lifted up the serpent in the wilderness, so must the Son of Man be lifted up, that whoever believes in him may have eternal life. (John 3:9–15)

_____

_____

_____

_____

_____

SHARING YOUR STORY

Every word contained in Scripture is flawless (Proverbs 30:5). What is your favorite verse (or verses) from the Bible? What has it meant to you? And how did it come to mean so much to you?

_____

_____

_____

_____

What verse (or verses) would you want _____ to remember? Why?

_____

_____

_____

_____

✎ Proverbs Thirty-One

Guided Tour

The last chapter of Proverbs is also the final major division of the book: "the sayings of Lemuel, a king" (31:1). This chapter deals with two major concerns shared with the king by his mother: wisdom for rulers (31:2–9) and wisdom for wives (31:10–31). The first section (31:2–9) begins, as the book of Proverbs does, with a summons to listen to wisdom (cf. 31:2 with 1:8ff.). After this introduction, the queen mother gives wise counsel to her son, the future king: Don't let women sap the strength of your reign (31:3) and don't let wine jeopardize the justice of your rule (31:4–7). Instead, a king should vigorously uphold the rights of the poor and powerless (31:8–9). Then in the second section (31:10–31), the queen mother commends to her son the qualities of a good wife. Her description, using an acrostic that features letters of the Hebrew alphabet (*aleph*, *beth*, etc.), paints the portrait of a strong, highly capable woman, who calls to mind the virtues of Lady Wisdom (Proverbs 1, 8, 9). In contrast to the "women" mentioned earlier in this chapter (31:3), who would drain the vitality of the king, the wise woman featured here enriches and strengthens her husband (31:11–12, 23, 28) as well as her entire household (31:11– 28). Her conduct reflects wisdom. She rightly relates to industrious labor (31:13, 17, 19, 27); money (31:16, 18, 24); people (31:12, 15, 20, 25, 26, 28); food (31:14–15); planning (31:16, 18, 21, 25); creation (31:13, 16); and initiative (3:13, 15, 16, 19, 24). Just as the woman in Genesis 1–2 stood as the high-water mark of the Creation narrative, so the woman of Proverbs 31 is the capstone of the wisdom extolled throughout the book of Proverbs. And as with all wisdom, her skillful and praiseworthy life stems from "the fear of the LORD" (31:30–31).

AT-A-GLANCE

31:1	Introduction
31:2–9	Wise Counsel for Rulers

[1] The sayings of Lemuel, a king—
an oracle that his mother taught him.

[2] Listen, my son! Listen, son of my womb!
Listen, son of my vows!
[3] Do not hand over your strength to women,
and your sovereign power to those who destroy kings.
[4] It is not for kings, Lemuel, not for kings to drink wine,
nor for rulers to crave intoxicants;
[5] lest he drink [them] and forget what is decreed,
and lest he change a verdict for every oppressed person.
[6] Let intoxicants be given to the one who is perishing,
wine to those who are bitter;
[7] let him drink and forget his poverty,
and remember no more his misery.
[8] Open your mouth for the mute;
to give judgment for everyone fading away.
[9] Open your mouth, judge righteously,
and issue edicts for the poor and needy.

[10] *aleph* A valiant wife who can find?
Her price is far beyond corals.
[11] *beth* The heart of her husband trusts in her;
he does not lack "spoil."
[12] *gimel* She does him good and not evil
all the days of her life.
[13] *daleth* She selects diligently wool and flax,
and works with her glad palms.
[14] *he* She becomes like trading vessels;
she brings her food from afar;
[15] *waw* and she arises [like a lioness] while it is still night,
and provides "prey" for her household,
and the quota [of food] for her servant girls.
[16] *zayin* She considers a field and purchases it;
from the fruit of her palms she plants a vineyard.
[17] *heth* She girds her loins with strength;
she strengthens her arms for the task.

¹⁸ *teth* She perceives that her trading is good;
   her lamp [of prosperity] does not go out at night.
¹⁹ *yodh* Her hands she holds out to the doubling spindle;
   her palms grasp the spindle.
²⁰ *kaph* Her palm she spreads out to the poor,
   and she holds out her hands to the needy.
²¹ *lamedh* She is not afraid for her household on account of snow,
   for all her household is clothed with scarlet.
²² *mem* Coverlets she makes for herself;
   her clothing is fine linen and [wool dyed with] purple.
²³ *nun* Her husband is respected at the city gate
   when he sits with the elders of the land.
²⁴ *samekh* Garments she makes and sells [them];
   sashes she supplies to the merchants.
²⁵ *ayin* Strength and majesty is her clothing,
²⁶ *peh* Her mouth she opens with wisdom,
   and loving teaching is on her tongue;
²⁷ *jadeh* one who watches over the affairs;
   the food of idleness she does not eat.
²⁸ *qoph* Her sons arise and pronounce her blessed;
   her husband [rises] and praises her:
²⁹ *resh* "Many daughters do valiantly,
   but you surpass all of them."
³⁰ *shin* Charm is deceitful and beauty is fleeting;
   as for a woman who fears the LORD, she should be praised.
³¹ *taw* Extol her for the fruit of her hands,
   and let her works praise her in the gates.

 Reflections

IDENTIFYING A VERSE

Write out the verse that stood out to you from chapter 31.

_____

_____

_____

Why did it stand out to you?

_____

_____

GOING DEEPER

Paraphrase Proverbs 31:30 into your own words of instruction to the future owner of this journal.

_____

_____

_____

What are some reasons why you think "charm" is identified as "deceptive" (NIV)?

_____

_____

_____

Why do you think "beauty" is identified as "fleeting" (NIV)?

_____

_____

_____

Take a moment to read about "the fear of the LORD" in "The Bird's-Eye View of Proverbs" (page 9). Why do you think the woman who "fears the LORD," in contrast to a woman merely possessing charm or beauty, is worthy of admiration and commendation?

_____

_____

_____

Over the years, where have you observed the truths of Proverbs 31:30?

_____

_____

_____

_____

CONNECTING THE GOSPEL

Read Proverbs 31:8–10, 29 and 2 Corinthians 12:9–10 (below). No king and no woman could consistently display the strength and excellence commended in this chapter. In light of this reality, what encouragement does 2 Corinthians 12:9–10 provide for times when strength and capacity fail?

_____

_____

_____

_____

PERSONALIZING A PRAYER

Write out a prayer for yourself and _____ using Proverbs 31 and 2 Corinthians 12:9–10. In your prayer reflect on the wisdom for every area of life that Proverbs outlines. As you think about your life and the life of _____ pray for "the fear of the LORD" that is the beginning of wisdom. Pray also that you will both know the grace of the Lord Jesus Christ that comes to us in our weakness and makes us wise like him.

> But he said to me, "My grace is sufficient for you, for my power is made perfect in weakness." Therefore I will boast all the more gladly of my weaknesses, so that the power of Christ may rest upon me. For the sake of Christ, then, I am content with weaknesses, insults, hardships, persecutions, and calamities. For when I am weak, then I am strong. (2 Corinthians 12:9–10)

_____

_____

_____

_____

SHARING YOUR STORY

Proverbs 31 gives wise advice about seeking a spouse (31:3). If you are married, what attracted you to your spouse in the early days of your relationship? How has this grown or developed over the years?

_____

_____

_____

_____

What's the best marriage advice you have received?

_____

_____

_____

_____

What advice would you give the recipient of this journal on his or her wedding day?

_____

_____

_____

_____

What qualities or practices should the recipient of this journal seek to adopt and live out as a husband or wife?

_____

_____

_____

_____

As you finish this journal, write down at least one thing you have learned from your study of Proverbs and would like to highlight for _____.

_____

_____

_____

_____

_____

_____

_____

_____

_____

_____

_____

_____

_____

_____

Acknowledgements

I thank the Lord for the opportunity to study the book of Proverbs and write about it for others. Many individuals have helped me during this project. Special thanks go to several friends: to Shannon Brown for his unflagging encouragement about this project over the last three years, and to Dr. Phil Brown, Dr. Curtis Hill, Wayne Robinson, Jeff Geshay, Marty Machowski, and to my father, George Thornton, for taking time to review an early draft and offer many helpful suggestions.

Additionally, I appreciate the kindness of both Dr. Bruce Waltke and Wm. B. Eerdmans Publishing in giving permission to use his excellent translation of Proverbs. I also want to express gratitude to Logos Bible Software for generously providing the tools I used to create the Topical Index.

This book would never have existed without the support of New Growth Press. I'm grateful for the leadership and vision of Karen Teears, and the top-flight editorial skills of Barbara Juliani and Gretchen Logterman. I have dedicated this book to George Thornton (my dad) and Eric Sipe (my mentor)—both men have poured into my life the fatherly wisdom they've learned from the Lord. It's my prayer that I, along with all readers of this book, may continue to receive the wisdom of Proverbs and pass it on to the next generation.

Endnotes

[1] This four-part pattern for prayer is based on a structure developed by Thomas Cranmer (1489–1556). Cranmer proposed five sections in prayer: (1) The Address; (2) The Acknowledgment; (3) The Petition; (4) The Aspiration; and (5) The Pleading. See Paul F. M. Zahl and C. Frederick Barbee, eds., *The Collects of Thomas Cranmer* (Grand Rapids, MI: Wm. B. Eerdmans, 2006), x–xi.

[2] Before you give away this journal, you may also want to allow others to add their contributions too. For example, once you finish the journal, you may ask another person (e.g., your spouse, one of your parents, etc.) to go through it as well, adding their comments in a different colored ink in order to distinguish which comments belong to whom. Or you may want to simply invite others to write a personal letter to the journal's final owner, using the blank pages provided at front or back of the book.

[3] Thomas Schreiner, *The King in His Beauty: A Biblical Theology of the Old and New Testaments*, (Wheaton, IL: Crossway, 2013), 282. "In some ways, Proverbs can be understood as an unpacking of the fifth commandment, which calls upon children to obey their parents."

[4] The two-line proverbs which dominate chapters 10–15 most often come in the form of "antithetic" or "opposing" parallelism, in which the first line is contrasted with the second line of the proverb. (E.g., 10:2, "Treasures gained by wickedness do not profit, but righteousness delivers from death.") The individual proverbs pervading chapters 16–22 feature more "synthetic" or "advancing" parallelism, in which the second line supports or enhances the thought of the first line. (E.g., 18:10, "The name of the LORD is a strong tower; the righteous man runs into it and is safe.")

[5] James Sire, *The Universe Next Door*, 5th ed. (Downers Grove, IL: InterVarsity Press, 2009), 20.

[6] Timothy J. Keller with Katherine Leary Alsdorf, *Every Good Endeavor: Connecting Your Work to God's Work* (New York: Riverhead Books, 2012), 215. "According to the Bible, wisdom is more than just obeying God's ethical norms; it is knowing the right thing to do in the 80 percent of life's situations in which the moral rules don't provide the clear answer. There is no biblical law that tells you what job to take, whether to go back to school, whom to marry and befriend, when to speak out or hold your peace, whether to make the deal or walk away—yet the wrong decisions can blow up your life."

[7] William J. Dumbrell, *The Faith of Israel: A Theological Survey of the Old Testament, 2nd ed.* (Grand Rapids, MI: Baker, 2002), 273. "True wisdom depends on an understanding of God's purposes in creation, which have

been particularized, as we know, in salvation history. Whereas prophecy reflected upon and responded to salvation history, the wisdom movement directed its attention to what creation itself implied for human conduct. In this sense, God's providential government of the world intersects with salvation history (i.e., God's special relationship to Israel)."

[8] Eugene H. Peterson, *A Long Obedience in the Same Direction*, 2nd ed. (Downers Grove, IL: InterVarsity Press, 2000), 120. According to Peterson, the "fear of the LORD" concerns these questions: "Will we let God be as he is, majestic and holy, vast and wondrous, or will we always be trying to whittle him down to the size of our small minds, insist on confining him within the boundaries we are comfortable with, refuse to think of him other than in images that are convenient to our lifestyle?" Alternatively, professor Philip Brown describes the "fear of the LORD" as the "compass of knowledge that orients it properly to the true North (Yahweh). Without that compass, one may know, but the orientation of that knowledge is misaligned to self, resulting in self-centeredness and selfishness which lead to self-destruction and harm to others" (from personal correspondence, January 2015).

[9] James Hamilton, *God's Glory in Salvation through Judgment* (Wheaton, IL: Crossway, 2010), 293, 295. "Like Exodus and Deuteronomy, Proverbs tells its audience that the fear of Yahweh is a guardrail that keeps travelers from going over the precipice to destruction. . . . The way of wisdom is not some recipe for the good life that has no reference to knowing and trusting God. The fear of Yahweh is its beginning (Prov. 1:7), and he is to be wholeheartedly trusted and known throughout one's ways (3:5–6)."

[10] James Fleming, quoted in Albert Wolters, *Creation Regained*, 2nd ed. (Grand Rapids, MI: Wm. B. Eerdmans, 2005), 29. Schreiner, *The King in His Beauty*, 299. "What is personified as wisdom in Proverbs reaches its fullest and final fulfillment in Jesus Christ. Wisdom does not represent Christ in [Proverbs] 8:22, for it is pictured as something created. But typology always involves escalation, so that Christ fulfills and exceeds what is said about wisdom in Proverbs, since he is the wisdom of God (1 Cor. 1:24, 30; cf. Col. 2:3) and is wiser than Solomon (Matt. 12:42)."

[11] This means that God intends us to learn wisdom by observing our world, using Proverbs as a divinely inspired model for our own observations. Graeme Goldsworthy, "Gospel and Wisdom," in *The Goldsworthy Trilogy* (Carlisle, UK: Paternoster Press, 2000), 418, comments, "[God] has thus revealed to us what we need to know in order to interpret our own life's experience and the universe around us. Within the framework of revealed truth, we actively go out in pursuit of the understanding of life, learning from our experiences and from those of generations before us." Therefore, the personalized "Reflections" that you can add at the end of each chapter of this book fall in line with what God intended. We should pass along both the wisdom learned through

reading Proverbs, and also our own wisdom gained through personally observing our world.

[12] Proverbs specifically names several men as the human authors of this God-inspired and inerrant biblical book: Solomon (1:1; 25:1), Agur (30:1), and Lemuel (31:1). For more information, see Bruce Waltke, "The Book of Proverbs: Chapters 1–15" in *The New International Commentary on the Old Testament* (Grand Rapids: Wm. B. Eerdmans, 2004), 31–37.

[13] Peterson, *A Long Obedience*, 119–20. According to Peterson, wisdom means "we accept the announced and proclaimed truth that God is at the center of our existence, find out how has constructed this world (his creation), how he has provided for our redemption, and proceed to walk in that way."

[14] The definition of wisdom as "skill in relationships" comes from an introductory lecture on Proverbs by Bruce Waltke, recorded October 17, 2014 (available at https://www.biblicaltraining.org/proverbs/bruce-waltke). Timothy J. Keller defines wisdom as "competence with regard to the [complex] realities of life," quoting Gerhard von Rad, in *Walking with God through Pain and Suffering* (New York: Dutton Adult, 2013), 134.

[15] On the other hand, if someone denies that there is a God and a design in the universe, then life can work in any way someone wants. To be sure, if your child tries to understand how this world works without the "fear of the Lord," he may become street smart, but he'll always be moving against the internal architecture of God's good world. After all, foolish people may appear quite savvy, but they also display great folly and ignorance: in their morals, ethics, priorities, relationships, etc. And their end is destruction. But the fear of the Lord is the beginning of true wisdom.

[16] Regarding how we should mentor others to become wise, Trevin Wax writes: "It's not enough to hope that [those we disciple] will believe the same things, or behave the same way; we want to see them *reason forward* as Christians. Inculcating Christian doctrine and imitating Christian behavior only takes you so far. If that is all you strive for in discipleship, you may wind up with mindless mimicry instead of thoughtful imitation. Discipleship includes helping people learn the 'mind of Christ' (Phil 2:5). The mind of Christ helps us to respond to new circumstances with the humility and wisdom of the Savior who indwells us by His Spirit. Imitation in the Christian life includes the cultivation of wisdom from within a biblical framework, wisdom that leads to the right decisions when the circumstances are difficult. Passing on the capability of wise reflection is an important aspect of discipleship. Ignoring this responsibility is disastrous for the future of the church" (from https://blogs.thegospelcoalition.org/trevinwax/2015/12/10/the-missing-strand-in-much-of-our-discipleship/; accessed January 19, 2017; emphasis mine).

[17] Goldsworthy, "Gospel and Wisdom," 369–70, "While the Christian accepts his responsibility to search for knowledge, he knows that human effort, discovery, and reasoning cannot provide a comprehensive understanding of the universe. . . . [Only] God . . . [has] exhaustive knowledge and can therefore define for us what reality is. By the same revelation this God has told us all that we need to know in order to know truly."

[18] Peterson, *A Long Obedience*, 121. Peterson quotes H. H. Farmer: "If you go against the grain of the universe, you get splinters."

[19] Goldsworthy, "Gospel and Wisdom," 486, "The challenges to the perceptible order posed by Job and Ecclesiastes, do not in any way rule out the deed-outcome relationship of Proverbs. The proverbial literature is saying that despite the exceptions and the mysteries, there is a discernible relationship between lifestyle and outcome."

[20] C. Hassell Bullock, *An Introduction to the Old Testament Poetic Books* (Chicago, IL: Moody, 1988), 162. "It is inappropriate to treat the proverbs of this book as promises. They are theological and pragmatic principles. . . . We are inclined to accept [Proverbs 22:6] as a promise, but the proverb really states a principle of education and commitment. That is, generally speaking, when a child is properly instructed in the way of wisdom from an early age, he or she will persist in that way. If, of course, other genres of Holy Scripture set forth that truth as a promise, then it is appropriate to view the proverb in that manner, while acknowledging that the promissory element does not originate with proverbs. That is not their purpose."

[21] Compare Proverbs 25:6–7 with Luke 14:10; Proverbs 2:4–5 with Matthew 13:44; and Proverbs 25:21 with Matthew 5:44; etc.

[22] Goldsworthy, "Gospel and Wisdom," 523. "The redemptive work of God, for the benefit of a sin-laden creation, was achieved not only by an atoning death, but by the new creation in Christ's person where God, man, and the created order are perfectly related."

[23] Ibid., 351. "The gospel, the message of the cross, is the wisdom of God for it is his way of restoring all relationships."

[24] This concept ("Do good? Get good.") was brought to my attention in J. D. Crowley's *Commentary on Romans for Cambodia and Asia* (ASEAN Bible Commentary Series) (Kindle Locations 230-231) (Fount of Wisdom Publishing House, Phnom Penh) Kindle Edition, 2014.

[25] Keller, *Every Good Endeavor*, 217. "The New Testament calls the Holy Spirit the 'spirit of wisdom' (Ephesians 1:17) and 'power' (1:19). Paul prays for his friends that God would fill them with "all the wisdom and understanding that the Spirit gives' (Colossians 1:9). . . . To be wise is to know how to best use every moment strategically. And this insight comes from the influence of the Holy Spirit, who also strengthens us to live a

life worthy of the Lord (Colossians 1:11) and is referred to as a 'spirit of power, of love, and of self-discipline' (2 Timothy 1:7)."

[26] Goldsworthy, "Gospel and Wisdom," 528–29. "By Christ, God is interpreting the meaning of the universe, of our world, and of the whole history of the human race. Christ interprets you and me so that we do not have to flounder in the ambiguity of our existence. He reveals to us what we need to know in order to get on with the business of living as responsible Christians."

[27] Ibid., 340–41, 343. "To think Christianly with a sanctified mind is to think of reality in terms of the truth that is revealed in Jesus. . . . The person and work of Jesus provide us with the only reliable basis for understanding ourselves, our experience, and the world."

[28] This four-part pattern for prayer is based on a structure developed by Thomas Cranmer (1489–1556). See endnote 1 for more information.

For Further Study

The following books may be helpful to use either at the present (while you work through this journal) or in the future (as you continue to study Proverbs).

Study Bibles

D. A. Carson, ed., *NIV Zondervan Study Bible* (Grand Rapids: Zondervan, 2015). Notes on Proverbs are coauthored by Bruce Waltke and Christopher B. Ansberry.

Wayne Grudem, ed., *ESV Study Bible* (Wheaton, IL: Crossway Bibles, 2008). Notes on Proverbs are coauthored by Duane Garrett and Kenneth Laing Harris.

General Overviews

Graeme Goldsworthy, "Gospel and Wisdom," in *The Goldsworthy Trilogy*, (Carlisle, UK: Paternoster Press, 2000), 329–550.

Derek Kidner, *The Wisdom of Proverbs, Job, and Ecclesiastes: An Introduction to Wisdom Literature* (Downers Grove, IL: InterVarsity Press, 1985).

Tremper Longman, III, *How to Read Proverbs* (Downers Grove, IL: InterVarsity Press, 2002).

Dan Phillips, *God's Wisdom in Proverbs* (Woodlands, TX: Kress Biblical Resources, 2011).

Topical Collections

Barbara Decker, *Proverbs for Parenting: A Topical Guide for Child Raising from the Book of Proverbs* (Boise, ID: Lynn's Bookshelf, 1989).

Donald Orthner, *Wellsprings of Life: Understanding Proverbs* (Greenville, SC: Emerald House Group, 1999).

Stephen Voorwinde, *Wisdom for Today's Issues: A Topical Arrangement of the Proverbs* (Philadelphia, PA: P & R Publishing, 1996).

Individual Commentaries

Duane Garrett, "Proverbs, Ecclesiastes, Song of Songs" in *The New American Commentary* (Nashville: Broadman Press, 1993).

Derek Kidner, *The Proverbs: An Introduction and Commentary* (London: Tyndale Press, 2009).

John Kitchen, *Proverbs: A Mentor Commentary* (Fearn, UK: Mentor, 2006).

Tremper Longman, III, "Proverbs" in *Baker Commentary on the Old Testament Wisdom and Psalms* (Grand Rapids: Baker Academic, 2006).

Bruce Waltke, "The Book of Proverbs: Chapters 1–15" in *The New International Commentary on the Old Testament* (Grand Rapids: Wm. B. Eerdmans, 2004).

Bruce Waltke, "The Book of Proverbs: Chapters 15–31" in *The New International Commentary on the Old Testament* (Grand Rapids: Wm. B. Eerdmans, 2005).

Topical Index

Note: In the "Bird's-Eye View of Proverbs" (pages 12–13), wisdom is defined as "living in right relationship with the realities of God's good and orderly, but fallen and chaotic universe. This includes properly relating to God, other people, the created world, and one's self." The Topical Index adapts this definition into five major categories: God, Creation, People, Self, and Wisdom. Thanks goes to the Bible software, Logos, for generously providing the digital tool, which enabled the topical tagging and labeling of almost every verse in Proverbs.

God

PERSON OF GOD

creator: 3:19–20; 8:22; 14:31; 17:5; 20:12; 22:2; 29:13; 30:4
defender: 20:22; 22:23; 23:11
holy: 15:29; 16:11; 30:3
judge & evaluator: 3:33–34; 5:21; 10:3; 12:2; 15:11, 25; 16:2; 17:3; 20:27; 21:2, 12; 22:12; 24:12, 18, 22; 25:22; 29:26; 30:6
loving: 3:11–12; 8:17; 15:9
pleasure & displeasure, his: 3:4, 32; 6:16; 11:1, 20; 12:22; 15:8, 9, 26, 29; 16:5, 7; 17:15; 20:10, 23; 21:3, 27; 22:14; 24:18
protector: 2:7–8; 3:11–12; 26; 10:29; 15:25; 18:10; 19:23; 22:12; 24:12; 30:5
provider: 8:35; 10:3, 22; 12:2; 15:29; 16:3; 18:22; 19:14, 17; 23:18
revealer: 2:5–6; 3:6; 29:18; 30:1, 4, 5, 6; 31:1
seeing: 5:21; 15:3; 20:27; 21:12; 22:12; 24:12
sovereign: 16:1, 3, 4, 7, 9, 11, 33; 20:22, 27; 21:1, 2, 30, 31; 25:2; 29:13
wise: 2:5–6; 3:19–20; 8:22; 19:21; 22:30; 30:2–4

RESPONSES TO GOD

fear of the LORD: 1:7, 29; 2:5; 3:7; 8:13; 9:10; 10:27; 14:2, 16, 26, 27; 15:16, 33; 16:6; 19:23; 22:4; 23:17; 24:21; 28:14
hearing: 13:13; 19:16; 28:9; 29:18; 30:5–6
obedience: 3:5–6, 11–12; 19:16; 28:13; 29:18

prayer: 2:3–4; 15:8, 29; 28:9; 30:1, 7, 8; 31:2
rebellion: 17:11; 19:3; 20:9; 21:4, 7; 24:9; 28:2, 13; 29:16, 18, 22; 30:9
trust: 3:5–6, 11; 14:32; 16:20; 18:10; 19:17; 20:22; 22:19; 28:25; 29:25, 26; 30:5
vows: 7:14; 20:25; 31:2
worship: 3:9–10; 21:3, 27; 28:5

Creation

ALCOHOL

20:1; 21;17; 23:20–21, 29–35; 31:4–7

BEAUTY & THINGS THAT ARE "FITTING"

6:25; 11:22; 19:10; 26:1; 31:21, 30

CONSEQUENCES & REWARDS

1:28–33; 2:7, 20; 3:2, 4, 6, 8, 9, 32; 4:12, 18; 6:9; 10:6, 29, 30; 11:3, 5, 8, 9, 17, 18, 21, 23, 27, 31; 12:1, 3, 7, 12, 21, 26, 28; 13:4, 5, 6, 12, 15, 20, 21, 22, 23, 25; 14:11, 14, 19, 34; 16:4, 5, 18; 18:3; 19:3, 19, 29; 20:7, 13, 17; 21:12, 13, 21; 22:3, 8, 25; 23:18, 21, 30; 24:16, 22, 25, 34; 26:26, 27; 27:12, 18; 28:10, 13, 14, 18, 20, 25; 29:5, 6, 16, 23, 25; 30:10, 33

IRONIES & MISTAKEN APPEARANCES

14:1, 3, 4, 5, 6, 7, 8, 9, 10, 11, 12, 13, 14; 16:25, 31; 17:1; 20:1, 3, 8, 14, 17

LIFE & DEATH

1:17–19; 2:20; 3:13; 4:10; 5:22; 6:12; 8:36; 9:18; 10:2, 16, 25, 27; 11:4, 19; 12:28; 13:9, 14; 14:12, 27; 15:10; 16:17, 25; 17:11; 18:7, 21; 19:16, 18, 23; 20:20; 21:16; 22:4, 5; 23:14; 24:20; 29:1; 30:17

NATURAL RESOURCES

abused: 6:9–11; 12:10; 18:9; 21:17, 20; 23:1, 3, 6, 20, 30; 24:15, 30, 33; 25:16; 26:14
cultivated: 12:10, 11; 13:23; 14:4; 21:20, 31; 22:9; 24:27; 27:23; 28:19; 31:13, 16
enjoyed: 12:27; 13:2, 4, 7, 11, 19, 21, 25; 24:4, 13; 25:16; 28:19
nature: 3:19–20; 6:6; 30:15, 18, 24, 29
society: 5:14; 31:23, 31

SEXUALITY

consequences: 2:18–19; 5:3, 8, 22; 6:26, 30, 34; 7:22, 26; 22:14; 23:27; 29:3
God's plan: 5:15–20; 12:4; 18:22; 19:14
temptation: 2:16–19; 5:3, 8; 6:24, 25; 7:6; 22:14; 23:14, 27; 30:20

TRIALS

adversity: 1:26–27; 3:22; 11:8; 12:13, 21; 13:17, 21; 14:32; 17:20, 23; 19:23; 24:10, 16; 25:19, 25; 27:10, 12
suffering: 9:12; 11:15; 13:20; 17:25–26; 31:6

WEALTH

22:1–4, 7, 16; 23:4; 28:6; 30:8
attitude toward: 3:9–10; 11:28; 13:7; 18:11; 22:1; 23:4; 28:22
bribes & gifts: 15:27; 17:8, 23; 18:16; 19:6; 21:14; 22:16; 25:14; 28:21; 29:4
generosity: 3:27–28; 11:24, 25, 26; 13:22; 19:17; 21:13, 26; 22:9; 28:27
greed: 1:13–14; 11:16, 26; 12:12; 14:30; 15:27; 28:22, 25
ill-gotten or corrupt: 1:16–19; 10:2; 11:18; 13:11; 16:8; 20:21; 21:6; 22:16; 28:8, 16, 20, 24; 30:9, 14
limitations of: 10:15; 11:4; 15:16, 17; 16:8, 19; 17:1; 19:1, 7, 22; 20:21; 21:9, 19; 22:2; 23:4; 25:24; 27:24; 28:6, 11
poverty: 6:9–11; 10:2; 11:24, 29; 13:8, 23; 18:22, 23; 19:1, 7; 21:5, 17; 22:2, 22; 23:21; 24:34; 28:6, 19, 22; 29:7; 30:8; 31:7, 8
results & effects: 10:15; 11:15, 24, 25, 28; 13:8; 14:24; 15:6; 19:4; 21:6; 22:7, 9, 16, 27; 28:11, 27
securing debts: 6:1–5; 11:15; 17:18; 20:16; 22:26; 27:13
source of: 3:9–10, 9; 8:18; 10:22; 15:6; 19:14

WORK

12:2–12; 14:1; 20:13; 22:29; 24:27
ambition: 16:26; 30:18
ethical behavior: 11:1; 20:10, 14, 17, 23; 22:28; 23:10
diligence & laziness: 6:6–8, 9; 10:4, 5; 12:14, 24, 27; 13:4; 14:23; 15:19; 18:9; 19:15, 24; 20:4, 13; 21:5, 25; 22:13; 24:30, 33; 26:13, 14; 28:19; 31:12, 13, 23, 31
employees: 25:13; 27:18; 29:19, 21; 30:23
employers: 26:10; 27:18; 29:19; 31:15

People

AUTHORITIES

honoring: 6:12–19; 22:11
limitations of: 11:7; 14:28; 21:1, 18; 27:24; 29:9
living under: 6:12–19; 14:35; 16:13, 14, 15; 18:16; 19:6, 12; 20:2, 26, 28, 30; 22:21, 29; 23:1; 24:21; 25:2, 3, 4, 6, 15; 28:12, 28; 29:2, 26
providing justice to wicked: 13:23; 16:10, 12; 17:15, 23, 26; 18:5; 20:8, 26; 21:15; 24:22; 29:4, 14; 31:4, 8
providing protection to poor: 17:26; 18:5; 22:22; 28:3, 15, 16; 29:14; 31:4, 8
wielding: 8:15; 16:12; 17:7; 18:17; 19:10; 25:2, 11; 27:23; 28:2; 29:4, 12; 30:22, 29; 31:3, 4

BROKEN RELATIONSHIPS

6:14, 19; 12:16; 13:5, 10; 14:20; 15:17, 18; 16:28, 29; 17:1, 5, 8, 9, 13, 14, 19, 27; 18:1, 3, 6, 18, 19, 21, 24; 19:4, 7, 13; 20:3, 19, 22; 21:7, 10; 22:10; 23:29; 25:16; 26:20; 27:3, 3; 28:25; 29:7, 22; 30:10, 14

FAMILY

17:1, 6; 19:7; 24:3; 27:8, 10; 31:15
children: 13:24; 14:26; 17:6, 21, 25; 19:13, 18, 26, 27; 20:7, 11, 20; 22:6, 15; 23:13, 24; 27:11; 29:15, 17; 31:28
father: 1:8; 4:3; 10:1; 11:29; 13:1; 15:20; 17:21, 25; 20:20; 23:22, 24, 25; 28:7, 24; 29:3; 30:11, 17
husbands: 6:34; 7:19; 12:4; 31:11, 23, 28
mother: 4:3; 10:1; 15:20; 17:25; 20:20; 23:22, 25; 28:24; 29:15; 30:11, 17; 31:1
wives & women: 5:15–20; 11:22; 12:4; 14:1; 18:22; 19:13, 14; 21:9, 19; 25:24; 27:15; 30:19, 23; 31:3, 10, 23

HEALTHY RELATIONSHIPS

discernment about friends: 1:15; 12:26; 13:20; 20:5; 22:24; 23:7; 24:1; 27:5, 11; 28:7; 29:24, 27
forgiveness: 17:9, 13; 19:11; 20:3; 24:29
helpful words: 27:6, 9
impartiality: 24:23; 28:21
influence of friends: 3:4; 13:20; 27:17

justice: 24:25, 28; 29:7
kindness: 11:16, 17; 14:21; 19:17; 21:13; 24:11; 25:21; 28:8; 31:12, 20
love: 10:12; 12:16; 15:17; 16:6; 17:9, 17; 20:28; 21:21; 30:19
loyalty: 16:6; 17:17; 18:24; 19:22; 20:6, 28; 24:21; 27:10
patience: 14:29; 15:18; 16:32; 19:11; 25:7, 15; 26:17
peacemaking: 3:29–30; 12:20; 17:14; 20:3; 29:8, 11
thoughtfulness: 21:29; 25:20; 27:14
trustworthy: 27:18; 28:20

OPPONENTS

2:12–15; 6:12, 17; 16:7; 18:17, 18; 24:17; 25:21, 22; 26:24; 28:10; 29:10, 13, 27
roots of: 24:24; 26:20; 29:10

RESPONSES TO DIFFICULT PEOPLE

the angry: 19:19; 22:24; 26:17; 27:11
the fool: 14:7; 16:22; 17:10, 12, 16; 23:9; 26:1, 3, 4, 6, 7, 8, 9, 10, 11, 12; 27:22; 29:9; 30:22
the gossip: 26:20–22
the guilty: 24:24, 25; 28:17
the liar: 26:23–28
the mischief maker: 26:17–19
the naïve: 1:4; 21:11
the proud: 16:19; 26:12
the mocker: 9:7, 8; 13:1; 14:6; 19:25, 29; 21:11; 22:10
the sluggard: 10:26; 26:13
the unfaithful: 25:19
the violent: 1:11–15; 3:31; 4:14; 26:25
the wicked: 1:10; 4:14; 9:7; 24:19; 25:4, 5, 26; 28:4, 28; 29:24

TEACHERS & PARENTAL INSTRUCTION

attitude toward: 1:7; 3:1; 4:20; 6:20; 7:1, 24; 9:8; 13:13; 15:12; 20:20; 23:26; 26:11; 27:7; 28:4; 29:1; 30:17
discipline of: 10:13, 17; 12:1; 13:18, 24; 15:5, 10, 32; 19:18, 20, 25; 20:30; 22:6, 15; 23:13, 14; 29:15, 17, 19
influence of: 4:3–9; 6:20; 7:5; 11:14; 13:14; 15:6, 7; 20:20, 29; 22:6
listening to: 1:5, 8; 2:1; 4:1, 10, 20; 5:1, 7; 6:20; 7:1, 24; 10:8, 17; 11:14; 12:15; 13:1, 10, 13, 14, 18, 20; 15:5, 12, 31; 16:20; 17:10; 19:20, 27; 22:17; 23:12, 19, 22; 24:6; 25:12; 28:4, 7, 9; 29:3; 31:2

VARIOUS PEOPLE

elderly, the: 10:27; 16:31; 17:6; 20:29; 22:6; 23:22
innocent & oppressed, the: 24:11; 29:7, 13; 30:14; 31:8, 9
messengers: 10:26; 13:17; 15:30; 25:13, 25; 26:6
neighbors: 3:27–28, 29; 6:3; 11:9, 12; 14:21; 21:10; 24:28; 25:7, 9, 16, 17; 26:19; 27:10; 29:5
outsiders: 5:10, 17; 11:15; 20:16; 27:2, 13
vulnerable, the: 14:31; 17:5; 18:23; 28:8; 29:13; 30:14; 31:8, 9, 20
young, the: 1:4; 7:7; 20:29; 30:19

Self

EMOTIONS

anger: 10:12; 14:16, 17, 29; 15:18, 20; 19:3, 19; 21:14, 24; 22:8; 27:3; 29:11, 22
confidence: 28:1; 31:21
contentment & peace: 5:19; 13:4; 27:8, 20; 29: 17; 30:7–9; 15–16
fear & anxiety: 1:33; 3:22; 12:25; 24:19; 29:25
guilt & shame: 3:35; 13:5; 18:3, 13; 19:26; 28:7, 17
hatred: 13:5; 24:9, 17
hope: 10:28; 11:7; 13:12, 19; 23:18; 24:14, 20
joy & happiness: 11:10; 12:20; 14:10, 13; 15:13, 15, 23, 30; 17:22; 18:20; 21:15; 23:15, 24, 25; 27:9, 11; 28:12; 29:2, 3, 6, 17
self-controlled: 16:32; 17:27
sorrow: 14:10, 13; 15:13, 15; 17:21, 22, 25, 25; 18:14; 23:29; 29:2; 31:6

INTEGRITY & RIGHTEOUSNESS

1:3; 2:20; 3:32, 33; 4:18, 26; 10:9; 11:3, 5–6, 10, 18, 20, 31; 12:3, 7, 12, 21, 28; 13:5, 6, 9; 14:9, 11; 15:9; 16:8, 11, 17, 31; 20:7, 9, 11; 21:3, 3, 8, 21; 22:11; 25:9, 26; 28:1, 6, 10, 13, 18; 29:2, 6, 10, 27

PERSONAL OUTLOOK

desires & hopes: 3:31; 6:25; 10:24, 28; 11:6, 7, 23; 13:2, 4; 21:10, 17, 25, 26; 22:1; 23:2, 3, 6, 17, 18; 24:1, 19; 27:20; 29:17; 31:25
heart: 4:23; 6:18; 7:25; 12:20, 23; 13:12; 14:10, 13, 30, 33; 15:7, 13, 14, 15, 28, 30; 16:23; 17:3, 20, 22; 18:12; 20:5, 9, 27, 30; 21:2, 4, 27; 22:15, 18; 23:12, 15, 19, 26; 24:2, 12; 25:3; 26:22, 23, 24, 25; 27:11, 19; 28:14
humility: 11:2; 12:9; 15:33; 16:19; 18:12

source of: 16:23; 27:21
tactful: 10:32; 15:1, 2, 4, 23, 28; 26:4
talkative: 10:8, 10; 18:2, 13; 20:19; 24:7; 29:20
teaching & wisdom, of: 10:13; 12:15; 18:4; 20:15; 22:18; 23:16; 25:11; 31:26
value: 10:20; 12:14, 19; 13:2; 16:24; 18:20; 20:15; 25:11, 25; 31:8

Wisdom

gaining: 1:2, 3, 20; 2:9; 3:13; 4:6; 8:4, 32; 15:32; 16:20, 23; 18:15; 19:8, 20, 25; 21:11; 22:15, 17; 23:23; 24:7, 14, 32; 28:5; 29:15; 30:3
knowledge & understanding: 1:4; 2:9-10; 10:14; 11:9; 13:16; 14:6, 18; 15:7, 14; 16:21; 19:2; 22:20
limitations of: 25:27; 26:7, 9; 30:18
personification of folly: 9:13–18
personification of wisdom: 1:20–33; 8:1–34; 9:1–6
protecting: 3:1, 3, 18, 21; 4:6, 13, 20; 5:2; 7:4; 13:15; 15:24; 17:24; 19:8, 27; 21:16; 22:3; 23:23; 28:26; 29:18
revealed: 2:5–6; 6:6; 8:4, 32; 9:10; 29:18
seeking: 2:3–4; 8:17; 14:6; 15:14; 18:15; 20:18
superiority & beauty of: 1:9; 2:9; 3:13; 8:6, 12; 9:13; 10:23; 11:22; 12:8; 16:16; 24:14; 29:3
value of: 1:2–6; 2:11, 12, 16; 3:13, 22, 35; 4:6, 12; 7:5; 8:6, 12, 32; 9:6, 11; 11:30; 12:1, 28; 13:15; 15:21; 16:16, 22; 17:2; 18:4; 19:8; 20:15; 21:16, 22; 22:3, 12, 19; 24:4, 5, 14